The
Bird-watchers' Book

Compiled and Edited by
JOHN GOODERS

DAVID & CHARLES

NEWTON ABBOT   LONDON
NORTH POMFRET (VT)   VANCOUVER

ISBN 0 7153 6669 6

Library of Congress Catalog Card Number
© John Gooders 1974

Set in 11 on 13pt Imprint and printed in Great
Britain by Latimer Trend & Company Ltd
Plymouth for David & Charles (Holdings)
Limited South Devon House Newton Abbot
Devon

Published in the United States of America by
David & Charles Inc North Pomfret Vermont
05053 USA

Published in Canada by Douglas David &
Charles Limited   3645 McKechnie Drive
West Vancouver BC

Contents

The adventures of a six-man Wildfowl Trust–Macmillan expedition to Spitsbergen in July 1973, to study the summer habits and biology—including the flightless period—of the Barnacle Geese which winter on the Wildfowl Trust Reserve and the neighbouring National Nature Reserve at Caerlaverock on the Solway Firth

How many different birds is it possible to record in Britain in one day? The author has several times managed 120 species, finding mid-May and coastal East Suffolk a successful blend of time and place. The pursuit is challenging, heightens one's powers of observation and provides an incentive to pinpoint scarce or localised breeding species

CONTENTS

Illustrations

ILLUSTRATIONS

All the photographs in this book have been supplied by Ardea Photographics, with the exception of those on pp 17, 18 (top), 53 (top), 126 (bottom), 143 (top).

Introduction

Like other areas of knowledge, the science of ornithology is expanding at the most incredible rate. There is more money for research, more field teams, more expeditions and more PhDs. Unfortunately the ornithological media for communicating the results of all this high-powered effort to others have not kept pace. The result is that authors seeking publication of a paper have frequently to wait for over a year to see their work in print. When papers are eventually published they are often so incomprehensible that their only raison d'être seems to be to communicate with the only other two or three people in the world who care. The latter are usually rivals and the major aim in publishing seems to be to forestall them. Of course, there are important papers buried among all this debris, but they are expensive to obtain and difficult to understand.

It has always seemed to me that a digest of knowledge about birds, written by the people doing the job, would be most valuable. And so the idea of a birds' annual was born. Our aim is to publish significant but interesting and readable articles by the best bird writers we can find. A glance through the list of contributors should be sufficient to convince anyone that we have succeeded. There's not much that's dry or dull in this book.

The Bird-watchers' Book will offer a varied bill of fare to suit all tastes, but it will never be just a rag-bag. In this first edition we have professional zoologists and enthusiastic amateurs among our contributors on subjects as far removed as 'fossils' and 'lifers'. But there is a bias—towards wildfowl and bird-watching. Next time we shall lean in another direction to bring you the top names in other areas of birds. Maybe it will be seabirds or garden birds—we shall just have to wait and see. But over the years *The Bird-watchers' Book* will grow into a veritable library of ornithology occupying a prominent place on your bookshelves and one that you will return to over and over again. In fact, of course, like all good things *The Bird-watchers' Book* can be savoured throughout the year.

Sussex 1974   J.G.

The land that God forgot

E. E. Jackson

The six-man Wildfowl Trust–Macmillan expedition sailed
north from Bergen on MS *Nordnorge* on 7 July 1973. Ahead
lay a six-day voyage through magnificent Norwegian coastal
scenery and out across the Greenland Sea to Spitsbergen. It
was an unforgettable journey blessed for much of the time
with perfect weather and with no hint of harder times ahead.
Most of our time was spent bird-watching from the boat,
going ashore from time to time to make brief sorties on Norwegian soil to add to our tally of birds. The list progressed
slowly and predictably, with few surprises but with some
moments to remember—like the magnificent spectacle of a
Peregrine mobbing a Sea Eagle in a series of breath-taking
swoops. At Alesund, hundreds of Kittiwakes nested on the
buildings around the harbour and even along the streets.
There was a great cacophony of sound in the enclosed space
which must prove trying to the other residents.

Sailing out of the spectacular Troll Fjord we spotted a
pine marten, or was it a polecat? We never could be sure, and
later on, near to the North Cape, we saw reindeer seeking food
on apparently barren mountainsides.

Cold Penetration

It was not without some foreboding that we sailed from the North Cape for Bear Island. We had crossed the Arctic Circle some two days before and we were now heading for one of the world's more notorious sea crossings. A storm was forecast but there was no need to worry. The sun shone all night, and the sea was calm. In the morning we sailed into fog, formed as the warm air of the Gulf Stream met the colder winds from the Arctic, and suddenly we felt as though we had arrived. There was persistent penetration in the cold, even without much wind, which sent us looking for our arctic clothing. The seabird cliffs on Bear Island are legendary for their enormous numbers of birds: Guillemots, Brunnich's Guillemots, Kittiwakes and Fulmars—millions of birds thronging round in that ceaseless frenzied activity so characteristic of seabird colonies. For sheer savage desolation Bear Island stands unique. A radio and meteorological station is permanently manned on the island for the benefit of boats which need to operate in arctic waters, and we stopped for a while to drop off needed supplies.

We arrived at Hornsund, 77° N in south-west Spitsbergen, at about 0400 hours on 12 July. The skipper of the *Nordnorge* had kindly agreed to deviate from the normal route to drop our party at Hornsund if conditions permitted. Much of the success of the expedition depended on our getting ashore here, for we believed this to be the centre of the Barnacle Goose breeding area. Despite a heavy swell we prepared to land. Our two 15 feet fibreglass dinghies were lifted out of the hold, the outboards attached and, with one man aboard, lowered over the side. Our equipment was lowered by the derrick into the boats, rising and falling with the swell. This was a dangerous and frightening experience. We had to unload almost two tons of equipment and almost every package threatened to go either through the bottom of the boats, or straight into the sea. More by luck than good management we were all finally ashore by 0730 hours.

Polish Hospitality

No more than three hundred yards from where we had landed was a hut built by the 1957 Polish Expedition as part of the International Geophysical Year programme. We had no previous knowledge of its existence and were naturally surprised and delighted with the shelter it offered. We were even more surprised to find the Polish flag flying outside and it turned out that, completely by chance, we had stumbled across the only other expedition in south-west Spitsbergen. A number of people were 'at home' and wasted no time in demonstrating the famous Polish hospitality. Breakfast was provided for us all, and space made available in the hut for us to share the accommodation. Several of the Poles spoke quite good English and we quickly became friends—they were mainly geophysicists and so our work programmes did not clash.

At Caerlaverock, Dumfries on the Solway Firth, there is a wintering population of some 4,000–5,000 Barnacle Geese. Here they spend practically all of their time on the Wildfowl Trust Reserve or on the adjacent National Nature Reserve. The Wildfowl Trust has pioneered a magnificent system of earth banks, covered approaches and hides which make it possible for large numbers of people to see and study the geese at close quarters. Much of the Trust's management of the reserve is dedicated to providing precisely the right conditions for the geese in order to keep them within sight of the hides, and detailed studies are made of the birds' feeding behaviour and preferences. The Caerlaverock Barnacles breed only in Spitsbergen. The Trust team had thus come to Spitsbergen to continue the winter studies and unravel more mysteries of the Barnacles' biology. We were also to make a film.

Within half a mile of base camp we found our first geese—four family parties of Barnacles grazing by a series of pools. Our first objective, however, was to visit the Dunoyane Islands, some ten miles north of base and two or three miles offshore. Overland journeys would obviously be slow because of the difficulty of the terrain and the problems of negotiating glaciers which ran straight into the sea. We had decided, therefore, that to remain mobile we would have to rely on the boats and trust to luck with the weather and sea.

Impressive Islands

The first journey to the islands passed without incident, though for the last mile the sea was very shallow and we were on constant watch for submerged rocks. The islands themselves have recently been designated as reserves by the Royal Norwegian Ministry of the Environment and access is now restricted. We had kindly been given permission to work on the islands and made several visits during the course of our stay. They were perhaps the most impressive islands that any of us had ever visited, and it really was a privilege to be there. The three Dunoyane Islands are low and flat, and not more than fifty feet high. Their shoreline is either shingle beach or rocky cliffs, and the sea around is strewn with skerries. In July their surface was covered with mosses, lichens, a few grasses and carpets of arctic flowers set in and around rocky outcrops and freshwater pools. In the background lay the

Page 17 (*above*) Eider Duck at nest, Spitsbergen, 1973; (*below*) a catch of flightless Barnacle Geese, including two white birds

Page 18   (*above*) Little Auks; (*below*) Nightjar

breath-taking panorama of the vast Torrellbreen Glacier and an endless range of snow-covered mountains. Barnacle Geese were nesting on the rocky outcrops, and of the twenty or so pairs we found on one island only two had hatched their young and the remainder were still incubating. The adult birds tolerated a fairly close approach, but later on when they had become flightless they were much more wary. Eider Ducks were very numerous with perhaps over a hundred nests on one island alone (see plate, p 17). We had no proof of breeding King Eiders but saw a few birds on the islands in addition to flocks of up to 180 non-breeding birds elsewhere. There were also nine Brent Geese but these too behaved like non-breeders.

To find Barnacle and Brent Geese as well as two species of eider was exciting enough for us—but there was much more. Red-throated Divers had young on the pools, Grey Phalaropes were nesting, and on one island was a flock of 160 moulting Long-tailed Ducks. Snow Buntings (the only passerines) were very common, as too were Purple Sandpipers. Both species were breeding, but the Sandpipers were already beginning to flock together for the southward migration. Turnstone, Ringed Plover and Whimbrel were also present and it seemed worth travelling all that way just to see the Turnstone in its startling summer plumage. The two predators on the island were the Arctic Skua—which seemed to take most of its food at the expense of a large Arctic Tern colony—and the Glaucous Gull. These gulls are positively evil! They are on constant watch for any bird which leaves its nest, and if any bird is foolish enough to do so even for a moment the gull swoops down immediately and takes whatever eggs or young have been exposed. By moving carefully we were able to prevent too much disturbance, but it is clear that if the islands are to remain the valuable sanctuaries they are at present, there must be no disturbance at all by visitors, at any rate until the young have been hatched off.

Flightlessness

The arctic summer is short. If the winter snows are a week or two late in clearing, there may hardly be time for the birds to complete their breeding cycle. Incubation and fledging periods are relatively short and in the case of the geese the annual moult has to be completed too. In most birds the main flight feathers are moulted one at a time so that the bird is always able to fly. But geese cannot afford the luxury of a protracted moulting period and all the flight feathers are moulted together in order to complete the process as quickly as possible. This means that they become flightless for a period —in the case of the Barnacle Geese, the flightless period seems to last for about three weeks. Breeding birds moult shortly after the eggs have hatched, the non-breeding birds a week or so earlier. Our expedition was timed to be in Spitsbergen during the period when the Barnacle Geese would be flightless, in order that birds might be caught and ringed (see plate, p 17). The object of ringing was not so much to learn about the birds' movements, but to mark the birds with specially made plastic rings which could be read at a distance. The birds could then be recognised as individuals and their fortunes within the flock followed over a number of years, without the necessity of recapturing them.

The largest concentration of Barnacle Geese which we found was about five hundred birds on the Dunoyane Islands. We had to wait for about a week for the breeding birds to be clear of their nest sites and then arranged for our first 'catch'. We were to adopt a technique used by a Norwegian party which had worked successfully on the islands ten years previously.

The selected island had to be approached quietly and the expedition members deployed at intervals around the shore line. At a pre-arranged signal everyone was to come up from the beach and show himself to the geese on the island. The geese, realising that they were surrounded, would then move on to a freshwater pond where they feel reasonably safe from intrusion, but from which they could, in fact, be easily caught.

Norwegian Technique

But what had worked ten years ago for the Norwegians was clearly not going to work for us. The first two attempts surprised no geese—indeed, on each occasion we were surprised to find that not only had the geese seen us coming, but they had left the island and swum about a mile out to sea. This was disconcerting because while we could approach the islands unheard by rowing the boats, with care, it was quite impossible to approach unseen with twenty-four hours of continuous daylight. The only alternative was to go out to sea and endeavour to fetch the birds back. Conditions were not ideal. The sea was littered with jagged skerries and ice floes, some visible some not, and strong currents provided additional difficulties. The geese too, seemed to know all about the hazards to small boats and led us through some quite hair-raising situations. We had come a long way to catch these birds though and we were not inclined to give up easily. Gradually we learned how to use our boat as a sheepdog and to drive the geese more or less where we wanted them. Before the drive started we had to predetermine the point on the beach where the birds would be landed. Four members of the expedition were strategically placed on the island, and as the geese were beached and ran away from the boat, they were surrounded, but allowed to run onto a freshwater pool. We now built a small holding pen with fifty yard guide walls on either side. If the geese were held on shallow ponds we could drive them into the pen quite easily by wading, but if the ponds were deeper we used inflatable dinghies. Once the geese were penned we were able to get on with processing.

Every bird was aged (if possible), sexed, weighed and the sternum and wing length measured. Two rings were fitted— the large plastic ring, specially made, and a standard metal ring, supplied by the Norwegian Ringing Office. In all we made half a dozen catches in various places and ringed a total of 416 Barnacle Geese. We used the technique described above except on two occasions when groups of adults and young were surprised on inland lakes. Towards the end of our stay many of the Barnacles were flying again and it was amazing how much less wary they became once the power of flight had returned.

Torrellbreen Glacier

We had established a camp on the mainland opposite the Dunoyane Islands at Hyttevika but after a couple of catches it was necessary to move on to a site further north. This involved crossing the twelve mile face of the Torrellbreen Glacier, which is constantly calving huge ice blocks into the sea and we clearly needed calm conditions for a safe journey. After a couple of days' wait the weather became settled, and the crossing was made without incident until we came to Kapp Borthen where our route took us through a narrow channel among a long line of skerries. The channel was boiling with the effect of opposing tides and currents and we had to beach the boats until the tide had turned and we could get through safely. We found a sheltered bay at Nebodden to harbour the boats and establish camp. There were 350

Long-tailed Ducks on the sea near to our camp when we arrived, but within a couple of hours fog had come down and we saw very little else for the next two days, while the weather demonstrated just how unpleasant it could be. Spitsbergen has been described as 'the Land that God Forgot', and at this time it was easy to see why. The beaches were littered with large quantities of drift wood, most of which had found its way to Spitsbergen from the rivers of Siberia, and we were able to cheer ourselves a little by building a temporary shelter and by lighting some impressive camp fires. Suddenly the weather cleared and we were able to resume our search for geese and make some of our most successful catches in this area.

The only Long-tailed Skua of the trip flew over our camp site at Nebodden, but we were surprised that it was in the company of three Great Skuas. These, the largest of the clan, are still uncommon in Spitsbergen, but we found two pairs holding territory (no actual evidence of breeding) and we were attacked quite vigorously by one pair. Later on, we heard that a Shetland-ringed Great Skua had been found further north by another expedition and it looks as though Spitsbergen will soon become another new area to be colonised by this rapidly increasing species.

Dovekies

For all of us there was no doubt that the bird of the expedition was the Little Auk or Dovekie (see plate, p 18). It was present wherever we went, quite literally in millions, nesting in the scree slopes running down from the mountains and among the boulders of the moraines. The largest concentration was by our camp at Hyttevika, where the constant racket of the auks' laughing calls made it almost impossible to sleep.

We did not mind since it was such a pleasure to see these delightful birds. They were every bit as engaging as the more familiar Puffins (of which we saw very few) and they kept us constantly amused by their antics. In a way they could be regarded as being responsible for the presence of many of the other birds and plants, since it is the Little Auk droppings which provide much of the nutrient for the plant regime, on which several birds, notably the geese, depend.

The Little Auks' only enemy seems to be the Arctic Fox. These charming animals were quite numerous around our base camp and came each evening for food which we put out for them. They were very inquisitive and showed little fear in approaching close to the battery of cameras which waited for them each night.

The return to base had been delayed by strong winds and we were lucky to get back when we did, for in the last week we had four days of almost continuous gale force winds blowing in turn from each point of the compass. The occasional Ivory Gull appeared during the storms, but our concern now was whether the sea would calm down sufficiently for the southbound steamer to pick us up.

The last day was blissful, calm and warm with brilliant sunshine. We ate our last meal of dehydrated food, and took the last of the 4,000 transparencies and mile and a half of film we were to bring back with us. The seas dropped as if by magic and shortly after midnight the MS *Kong Olav* came into the fjord to pick us up. It took only half an hour for us to get aboard—and into the bar. Before we had had our first drink two Storm Petrels flew close by the boat. They were the first ever recorded for Spitsbergen.

Big day in East Suffolk

David Pearson

How many species of birds is it possible to record in Britain in a day? Where and when can the highest counts be made? A varied and active day's bird-watching in late spring or early autumn could probably produce a hundred species in many coastal areas, but higher totals call for a certain amount of planning, plus careful selection of date, itinerary and, if possible, weather. It might be imagined the best results would be obtained by scouring as large an area as possible in some particularly fast vehicle, but hours spent on the road at fifty miles per hour represent hours lost in the field. Given a sufficiently productive and varied part of the country, there is much to be gained by confining efforts to a single county or smaller area, in which 'difficult' breeding species have been located in advance.

Mid-May

In recent years, P. A. Smith and I have several times attempted, in May, to list 120 species in a day in coastal east Suffolk, usually with success. Our area offers a wide variety of habitats and supports a particularly large number of breeding species. The middle of the month has proved the best time

25

for a count, with the last of the summer visitors just in, and the spring wader passage still in full progress. Success has been largely determined by the weather, for a warm still morning is essential for efficiently recording all the common woodland and hedgerow songbirds, while light easterly winds tend to increase the wader variety and are likely to produce other unexpected visitors.

Our first high count was made on 10 May 1959, when a coastal strip some twelve miles long by six miles wide was worked entirely by bicycle. A fine warm day which began with Bittern, Nightjar (see plate, p 18) and Nightingale at 0300 hours and included Woodcock, Long-eared Owl, Red-backed Shrike, Wood Warbler, Crossbill, Garganey and fifteen species of waders, finally ended after dark with Stone Curlew and Tawny Owl, 120 species and seventy-two miles later.

Target–120

This total was not to be substantially improved on for a number of years, but a new mark was set on 13 May 1965, during a fine week in which light easterlies brought in a good selection of spring waders. The aim on this occasion was to make sure of all the obvious species as early in the morning as possible. There is nothing more disastrous in the middle of the day than having to delay visits to likely wader spots to comb yet another wood for a missing Treecreeper or Marsh Tit. The main haunts around Blythburgh, Walberswick and Westleton were, therefore, thoroughly covered before break-fast by bicycle, the best form of transport for ensuring that common species, which should give no trouble, are all picked up quickly and efficiently.

We intended to account for as many nocturnal species as

26

possible before dawn, so that the dusk hours would give enough time to chase the few birds that still remained. After a brief pause within earshot of Westwood Marsh to start the day with Grasshopper Warbler and Sedge Warbler, our first quest was the pair of Long-eared Owls nesting in a pine wood outside Walberswick. Sure enough, a bird was calling away quietly in the treetops at 0230 hours. A Tawny Owl hooted nearby, and the distant Redshank calling was interrupted by the louder squeals of a Water Rail. Back at Blythburgh Fen half an hour later Nightingales were vocal, and the booming of a Bittern came from the direction of the marsh. In vain we listened for the sound of an early Nightjar. Had they arrived yet? A Skylark began to sing, and was soon followed by the many sounds of the early dawn chorus: Cuckoo, Song Thrush, Robin, roding Woodcocks, Woodpigeon, Redstart, Blackbird and Pheasant.

Bearded Tits and Marsh Harriers

By 0415 hours it was time to make a move to Westwood Marsh. Yellowhammer and French Partridge were quickly added, and the walk past the oak wood to the reedbeds pro-duced Shelduck, Great Tit, Willow Warbler, Goldcrest and Treecreeper. We emerged onto the marsh to be immediately greeted by the sounds of Reed Warbler (see plate, p 35), Waterhen, Snipe and Coot. A Heron rose with raucous call, and a group of Mallard took to the wing. A group of Swallows flew by and a party of Jackdaws passed overhead. A short excursion along a path into the reeds disturbed a pair of Bearded Tits, and put up a Teal and a party of Gadwall from a small mere. But of the normally resident pair of Little Grebes there was no sign. We waited hopefully, and were unexpectedly rewarded, for a pair of Marsh Harriers rose nearby and

27

commenced full display flight, the first breeding behaviour to be seen on the marsh that year. Meanwhile a group of Sand Martins and a lone Carrion Crow flew by. Finally, a whinnying call announced the presence of the Little Grebes, one of which obligingly swam into view.

It was now 0515 hours, under twenty hours to go and time to return to the heath. With the sun just up, and many more species in song, the journey back to the lane contributed Chiffchaff, Blue Tit, Garden Warbler, Chaffinch, Wren and Nuthatch. A few minutes were spent productively around some heath edge farm buildings and an adjacent copse: House Sparrow, Blackcap, Greenfinch, Mistle Thrush, Dunnock, Goldfinch, Tree Sparrow, Whitethroat, Spotted Flycatcher and Redpoll followed one another in quick succession, and a distant Green Woodpecker called to bring the total to 57 species.

The Fen had now to be revisited to take care of the remaining members of the tit family, and the short ride back accounted for Starling, Linnet and Stock Dove; two Green Woodpeckers took to the wing and the first Lesser Whitethroat of the morning sang vigorously from a clump of blackthorn. Tree Pipits were now in full display song around the Fen, and from within the wood came the sound of Turtle Doves and Coal Tits. A rather fruitless twenty minutes' walk into the depths of the wood added only Great Spotted Woodpecker, but efforts were eventually rewarded. A Marsh Tit condescended to break into a burst of late season song, and almost immediately afterwards, from the swampy undergrowth a few yards away, came the 'chaar, chaar, chaar' call of the Willow Tit known to be nesting in the vicinity. The list then received another unexpected bonus, for a sharp repeated call announced the presence of a Lesser Spotted Woodpecker as it disappeared high into some tall alders.

Rush of Species

With practically all the woodland and hedgerow species now accounted for, it was time to move on again, and investigate Walberswick shore. Meanwhile, would the Red-backed Shrikes be back at the traditional site near the village? Lucky again! A male, the first of the season, was perched prominently on the usual bramble bush. The ride along the dyke wall past the mill to the shore produced the expected rush of new species: Common Tern, Black-headed Gull, Little Tern, Lapwing, Mute Swan, Ringed Plover, Meadow Pipit and Yellow Wagtail. Two calling Whimbrel flew north overhead, and a quick glance at the shore pools showed the presence of an interesting scattering of waders. Discarding bicycles, we invested half an hour in the inevitable trudge along the shingle and back. In addition to the resident Oystercatchers and the expected small party or two of Dunlin, several Turnstone and a Common Sandpiper were seen together with a party of Grey Plover in full breeding plumage. Common Gulls and a Lesser Black-back flew north along the sea wall, and a Fulmar passed south, close inshore. As we set off again on bicycles, a Greenshank flew up from a small ditch calling loudly. Exactly 0700 hours and eighty-seven species up.

The temptation to fit in the shore and public hides at Minsmere before breakfast was now overwhelming, but first there were birds to be accounted for on Westleton Heath. The four-mile ride through Dunwich Forest added the expected Jay, but there was no sign or sound of a Long-tailed Tit. Outside Westleton, a quick pause at a likely Corn Bunting site was immediately rewarded by the hoped for 'bunch of keys' jangle. A relief, for this can be an exasperatingly difficult bird to find if it chooses not to sing. A mile further along the road to Dunwich a cock Stonechat sat prominently on the wires, and a quick scan with binoculars revealed a pair of Whinchats on the heather tops not far away. And so, on to Minsmere with not a Magpie or a Kestrel in sight, and every Partridge examined turning out to be a red leg!

RSPB Courtesy

Our hopes of a substantial boost by courtesy of the RSPB were not to be disappointed. Ensconced in the first public hide, with Sandwich Tern behind us, we were quickly able to list Canada Goose, Avocet, Herring Gull and Shoveler. The first Swifts of the morning fed over the trees at the back of the marsh, and an immaculate drake Garganey swam into view, a bird we had hoped for but by no means expected. Another Greenshank flew past, but the Spotted Redshanks all appeared to have left. However, the wader picture was brightened considerably by the appearance of first a Ruff, unusual on so late a date, and then, to bring the hundred up, a Kentish Plover. The journey back to a nine o'clock breakfast at Blythburgh Fen added Wheatear on Minsmere clifftop, and finally House Martin and a genuine English Partridge.

So far, with ten useful hours of the day left, the position was extremely encouraging, and the atmosphere of optimism was increased during breakfast by the appearance of a pair of Long-tailed Tits, churring in the hedge outside our cottage window. Why not, we wondered, a quick dash to the Breck or the north Norfolk coast? These evil thoughts were pushed aside, however. This was to be an east Suffolk count! After a suitable pause for rest and refreshment we transferred with some relief to motor transport, and the late morning session began fairly auspiciously with a Collared Dove in Walberswick village and a Pied Wagtail along the road to Blythburgh. Another easy addition was made as we passed the first

Rookery of the day en route for Easton, a few miles up the coast.

A scan with binoculars from Easton clifftop revealed little that would normally call for much comment, but on this particular day a small party of Scoter about half a mile offshore was an extremely welcome sight. A few hundred yards up the shingle beach, the muddy edges of the broad held an encouraging number of passage waders. More Greenshank, Grey Plover and Common Sandpipers were seen, but of more immediate interest were two immaculate Bar-tailed Godwits and three jet black Spotted Redshank. Further along the broad a rather uninspiring looking collection of resting immature gulls proved to contain a number of Kittiwakes, and a party of small waders flying north close inshore included two Sanderling.

Things were now going very well indeed. With the tide rising on the River Blyth there was just time for a look at the estuary and at least two certain additions to the list before lunch at the White Hart. Again, expectations were exceeded. Curlew, Great Black-backed Gull and Cormorant were quickly recorded, and attention was then turned to the assortment of waders concentrated by the tide in one corner of the mud flats. Included were Whimbrels, Bar-tailed Godwits, Grey Plovers, a Greenshank and, yes, a small party of Red Knot. Finally, feeding with Dunlin on an exposed strip of mud beside the river channel were two Curlew Sandpipers, one of them in full breeding plumage. One hundred and seventeen species by lunch!

Magpie Rarity

From now on things were not going to be easy. The euphoria of the early morning had already given way to the realisation that there were not all that many more species to look for, and not many useful new places to visit. Kestrel was still missing and as usual in May in this well keepered area Magpie remained elusive. Apart from two possible night species and a couple of 'certainties' on a lake a few miles inland, there were no easy omissions to rectify. One or two pairs of Woodlarks still bred near Westleton, and it was to a likely rabbit warren that we turned our attention after lunch. No Woodlarks could be flushed and it was only after a considerable time, when hope had almost run out that a single bird was spotted sitting quietly in a small tree.

Magpie was the next quest, and here again much valuable time was lost. Repeated and exhausting attempts were made to flush birds out of a traditional nesting site in dense blackthorn at Snape. Eventually a bird was sighted as it disappeared into a hedge several hundred yards away across the marshes. The next stop was Orford, the plan being to walk along the river wall towards Havergate Island in the hope of catching sight of one of the nesting Short-eared Owls. This proved unnecessary, for on emerging from the car at the quay almost the first thing we set eyes on was an owl which obligingly took to the wing on the peninsula immediately opposite.

The drive inland could no longer be postponed. On the way we finally set eyes on a Kestrel, the first, amazingly, in over twelve hours in the field. In the Waveney Valley, the anticipated Tufted Duck and Great Crested Grebe were duly added to the list at 1700 hours, together with a drake Pochard, a somewhat scarce bird in east Suffolk in the breeding season and an unexpected bonus. Perhaps the late afternoon could have been better spent hoping for a Spoonbill, a Black Tern or other more exciting vagrants at Minsmere, but we shall never know.

We were now too tired to respond to the temptation to

continue inland and finish the day in the Breck. One hundred and twenty-four species and definitely tea time, so we returned towards the coast, carefully scanning every telegraph pole and likely roadside elm for a Little Owl, but to no avail. After a pause for food and general recovery we again made for Westleton Heath, and positioned ourselves overlooking a wood where Sparrowhawks were thought to be nesting. After an hour in which no Hawks or other potential additions to the list made an appearance it began to seem as if that might be that, when just after sunset a Stone Curlew rose close at hand and flew round calling noisily. One more reasonable possibility remained, and sure enough, when hopes were fading rapidly with the light, the first Nightjar of the season began to churr a hundred yards away. Any Little Owls along the route home kept obstinately clear of the headlights, and so the final total for the day remained at one hundred and twenty-six.

Fun with a Purpose

With so challenging and enjoyable a pursuit, it is perhaps redundant to question the point of a once in a while 'big day's' tick list. We have been aware, however, of two useful functions served by our activity in Suffolk. Firstly, it has often provided an incentive to check on the whereabouts of scarce or localised breeding species, when nesting might otherwise have gone undetected in the coastal area in question. Secondly, it has served to emphasise marked local changes in the late spring status of a number of species over the last fifteen years. Sparrowhawk, Barn Owl, Little Owl and Kingfisher could all reasonably be expected during a day's bird-watching in May in the 1950s, while Stone Curlews, Whinchats, Wheatears, Woodlarks and Corn Buntings still bred commonly on many heaths during the years of our first counts. None of these

33

species can any longer be guaranteed on a daily May list unless a pair is carefully located beforehand. The last four had in fact ceased to breed at almost all their old coastal sites by 1970. There is a brighter side, however. The Collared Dove appeared as a common breeding bird during the early 1960s, while Redpoll, Avocet and Canada Goose, which were formerly scarce in May and difficult to list, could now hardly be avoided. With the recent establishment of disused gravel pit habitats, and the now regular breeding of such species as Black Redstart and Savi's Warbler, a number of birds can be counted on for a 'big day' which would have been considered most unlikely fifteen years ago.

Finally, on a different note, although we feel sure that with the use of a sports car, Land-Rover and, possibly, private light aircraft, someone must have clocked up 130 or even 140 species in Britain in a day, can any other county beat east Suffolk? We feel justified in laying tentative claim, at least, to the non-motor-assisted record!

Page 35 (*left*) Reed Warbler; (*below*) Goldfinch amongst thistleheads

Page 36 (*above*) Goldfinch nesting in an apple tree; (*below*) bird-watchers

A charming Goldfinch

Geoffrey Beven

The cheerful tinkling of a charm of Goldfinches flitting like butterflies over the thistle heads with a flash of black and gold wings, is nowadays quite familiar. This was not always so. In the nineteenth century the numbers of Goldfinches in Britain greatly decreased and the bird became comparatively scarce. By 1900 it was said to be virtually extinct in some districts. At that time the Goldfinch was a popular cagebird, which it still is over much of southern Europe. Not surprisingly the decrease was largely attributed to bird-catchers, who were undoubtedly taking large numbers. It has been stated, for example, that an average of 14,000 were caught annually in the Worthing area alone, while 144 were captured in one morning in Paddington. Public opinion became aroused and led to the Protection of Birds Acts (from 1880 onwards) and these seem to have effectively stopped much of the trade in native cage birds.

Subsequently Goldfinches became much more numerous again in England, southern Scotland and Ireland. However, it seems likely that the spread of the bird's food supply in the form of thistles and other weeds on neglected arable farmland following a decline in agriculture at this time, may have contributed to the increase. Around London in 1880 the bird had decreased from a comparatively common resident to one of the rarest breeding species. By 1908 there had been some recovery, but even in 1940 birds were seldom seen in central London. During the war they became more frequent on weedy patches, by bomb shelters and anti-aircraft guns, becoming more and more suburban birds, and in recent years they have nested increasingly in gardens.

Range Extension

The Goldfinch is now fairly numerous as a breeding bird in England, especially in the south, and in Wales and Ireland, but is more local in Scotland, reaching northwards to Perth and Inverness with occasional nests in Ross and Sutherland. Recently the range has extended in Ireland and it has colonised the Isles of Scilly. Likewise in southern Fennoscandia, during this century, a northward expansion of range has occurred into cultivated land, nesting being first recorded in Norway in 1955. Breeding also in Iberia, the range extends eastward through Europe to north-west Mongolia and the western Himalayas, while southward it extends to north-west Africa and the Middle East. Birds in the extreme eastern parts of the Asiatic range occur predominantly on mountains and have the crown grey, whereas this is black in the western birds; the two forms hybridise freely in parts of Iran and southern Siberia.

In autumn a large proportion of the British birds leave, mostly wintering in the Low Countries, France and Iberia, but some in Ireland, returning in mid-April and May. More hens than cocks migrate. In some autumns birds are observed arriving on the east coast of England, but it is still uncertain whether any of these are from the Continent. Very large numbers winter in the Mediterranean basin, especially in Iberia, where there is an almost continuous supply of seeds for them.

Feeding mainly on seeds, they appear to be able to survive most severe winters without disaster.

Introductions

Such a conspicuous and beautiful songbird would inevitably be introduced to other lands, and these include Australia, Tasmania, New Zealand, Argentina and Bermuda. It has settled well in most of these countries, becoming a common garden bird even in towns, but it did not succeed in North America, perhaps because of competition with the closely related American Goldfinch. In New Zealand, on the other hand, the Goldfinch has even become a pest through its habit of picking seeds from strawberries, and in Britain it has been incriminated as a destroyer of buds in orchards while seeking insects living in them.

The Goldfinch was well known in Mediterranean lands in the Middle Ages, being frequently represented in Italian religious paintings as a symbol of the Resurrection because of its gold wings; and its association with thistles, was linked with the crown of thorns. But it was also used as an augur of disease.

About 5 inches long, with a red face mask, white cheeks, and black crown and side stripes, the Goldfinch is one of Europe's most beautiful birds. The back and flanks are buff on chestnut, the rump and belly whitish. The wings are black with a broad yellow bar, each flight feather having white tips. The feathers of the black tail not only have white tips, but the two outer pairs have white patches on the underside. The whitish conical bill is rather long and narrow and has a black tip in winter. The female is smaller and duller than the male; and the juveniles, sometimes called 'grey pates', are streaked greyish-brown, have similar wings and tail to adults, but lack the red, white and black on the head.

Thistle Feeders

Goldfinches feed predominantly on thistles (see plate, p 35), probing deeply with the bill into the base of the thistle head to remove the fruits. In a recent important study Dr Ian Newton has pointed out that there are several structural adaptations to facilitate this method of feeding. The feathers of the red blaze on the face are particularly short and stiff, and probably help to resist the prickles and spines in the heads of the thistles and other food plants. Also, the beak is especially long and narrow for a finch, and is used like a pair of tweezers to pierce and probe into the tough seed heads in order to pick out the seeds embedded deeply. The bill opening muscles are strongly developed so that the bird can separate bracts of cones and open seed heads with a gaping movement. These adaptations enable the bird to feed extensively on thistles from mid-summer throughout autumn and winter. In addition it appears that the Goldfinch is the only British finch that can reach the seeds of the teazle, which, lying at the bottom of long spiked tubes are mainly taken by the males whose bills are, on average, one millimetre longer than those of the females. As a consequence, the females only take these seeds with difficulty. After the autumn moult the feathers of the blaze appear orange, becoming redder in a few weeks although remaining orange in many females.

'Chirms' to 'Charms'

In the breeding season the Goldfinch frequents cultivated areas such as parks, shrubby gardens, orchards, and clearings in broadleaved and coniferous woodland, feeding largely in open ground. In autumn and winter it moves to any waste ground with thistles and other weeds, allotments and neglected pastures. Parties of these birds used to be called 'chirms', meaning a chorus of sounds or chirps, but with a change of spelling the term became 'charms', and most suitably restricted to Goldfinches. With dancing flight they cover the thistle and weed beds, alighting daintily on the seed heads, passing quickly from one plant to another and keeping up a cheerful liquid twittering. Often they hang like tits, especially when on alders and birches they ransack the cones. When singing they tend to occupy the topmost branches of trees or suburban television aerials. Less often they may be seen on the ground, searching for alder seeds among debris left after flooding.

Goldfinches feed mainly on the seeds of the *Compositae*, especially thistles, but also dandelions, groundsels, ragworts, burdocks, daisies, docks and hardheads. Around Oxford, Dr Newton found that not only did thistles form one third of the annual diet, but also that the fallen heads of thistles and burdocks were preferred to those on the plants which then remained available later on when the ground was snow-covered. In spring pine cones are opened to extract the seeds, while beetle larvae may be picked from developing larch buds. On the other hand, the food given to the nestling is very different. It consists of a mixture of seeds and insects, including caterpillars and aphids, the proportion of seeds increasing as the young get older so that when about to fledge they are having seeds alone, mainly dandelion, groundsel and thistle.

Such agile feeders cling easily to vertical stems, often hanging upside down, almost all food being obtained directly from trees and herbaceous plants. When feeding from dandelions or other plants with short, weak stems, a bird alights about half way up and as its weight bends the stem it moves towards the seed head until this touches the ground, when it can remove the seeds. C. W. Craig observed a female repeatedly using a

different method to reach the seeds of dandelions which were
bending over water and, therefore, could not be brought down
to touch the ground in the usual way. She alighted and nipped
the stem, partly cutting it through, and then pulled the seed
head back towards her, gripped it with her feet, and ate the
seeds. She may not have quite realised why she was doing this,
maybe she did not climb further along the stem owing to
reluctance to go nearer the water, but she had clearly learned
enough to repeat the actions successfully.

When feeding the Goldfinch regularly uses its feet, especially
when extracting the seeds of birch and alder. It reaches down
for a birch catkin, pulls it up with its beak, then holds it against
the twig with its front toes while pecking. Even in the sixteenth
century bird fanciers called the Goldfinch the 'draw-water';
they found that birds in cages soon learned to pull up one string
holding a small container with food and another string with a
thimble of water, pulling the string with the beak and holding
it with a foot, and then repeating the process.

Small Territories

As the young birds are fed mainly on seeds, Goldfinches do
not need to depend for their food supplies on their very small
territories, which only include the immediate vicinity of the
nests. These are close together, often in loose colonies of
perhaps two or three pairs, possibly in the same tree. According
to Dr I. Newton, the function of this very small territory is to
isolate or space the pairs in a colony and minimise disturbance,
especially from other males. Suitable seed is often concentrated
in widely-spaced localities, which change as different plants
come into seed. The birds, therefore, may have to forage some
distance away, perhaps up to two miles. Where food is available
it is usually abundant, so that Goldfinches are able to remain in

parties throughout the year. In order to maintain the pair bond in these circumstances, there are mutual displays and the pair tend to remain together when foraging and bringing food to the nest. With their distensible gullets the birds are able to bring large meals to the young, which they visit at infrequent intervals, perhaps every ten to sixty minutes.

In early spring, while in the flock, the male finds a mate. Sexual chases occur in which the female is often dominant. Later the pair perform a 'pivoting' display. Here both birds crouch and swing from side to side about the legs, the wings being depressed to expose more yellow, the tail spread and red blaze expanded, while uttering a 'tu-wee-oo' call. A similar display is used aggressively when a cat approaches the nest. During courtship feeding, the cock regurgitates food into the open bill of the hen. There is also a 'moth' display flight in which the male flies near the female with rapid shallow wing-beats. Over open breeding areas there is a 'butterfly' song flight with a continued jumble of calls making up a cheerful tinkling song. The territory is established only after the nest site is chosen, although it may be defended by both sexes before the nest is made. When a new nest is built for a subsequent brood a new territory is defended, as the birds tend to move around and settle where food is plentiful.

Prisoner-of-War

When nesting, Goldfinches are sometimes remarkably tame. In 1943 P. J. Conder was able to watch, without a hide, three pairs at the nest at a range of 7 feet in a prisoner-of-war camp in Bavaria. He noted that one bird continued to incubate eggs in an alder while a crowd of prisoners stood watching football just beneath it. Nests are usually placed in conifers and deciduous trees in parks and orchards (see plate, p 36) high on a bough 12 to 30 feet up, but in Portugal they are sometimes in very small trees, perhaps only 4 or 5 feet from the ground. Placed often at the end of high branches, the nests sway violently in the wind and are thus probably safer from large predators. However, some nests are deserted or even blown down. The cup of the nest is usually quite deep and this no doubt helps to retain the eggs and young in these conditions.

In the early stages of nest construction there is a foundation platform of spider's web, the bird dropping a loose end over a branch and picking it up on the other side. Vegetable fibres and more spider silk increase the platform, which is moulded into nest shape by swivelling and trampling activities of the hen, who does all the building although the male keeps near her. The final structure is a neat and compact cup made of roots, moss, bark and lichens, wool and spider web, lined with down of thistles, dandelions and other plants. In southern England four to six whitish eggs with red-brown blotches are laid from mid-May right up until early August, and incubated by the hen for eleven to thirteen days, starting sometimes with the last egg but one. She sits day and night for up to 98 per cent of the incubation period, and is fed by the cock on or off the nest. When feeding young, the adults husk seeds and crush insects and then regurgitate a mass mixed with water and particles of grit. At first seeds are passed through the nestlings undigested and at this stage the faeces are eaten by the parents. Later the faeces are carried away, until the eighth day after hatching when nestlings begin to void over the edge of the nest, some faeces being characteristically left to accumulate on the rim. The young usually leave the nest at thirteen to sixteen days and then fly vertically upwards to the tree tops. At this time, when uneasy, they tend to alight on each others' backs, as if to experience again the reassuring close contact they have had while in the nest. The parents feed them for a further ten days, and these noisy family parties are typical sounds of weed beds in summer. The main losses of nests are from squirrels and various crows, as well as those due to high winds. There are usually two broods, sometimes three. Warm dry seasons with plenty of seed food enable many more young birds to be reared.

What is a
Bird-watcher?

John Gooders

It often interests people that I am a bird-watcher.

'Oh' they say, 'Do you know Peter Scott?'

'Yes' I reply, 'Why? Do you know him well?'

'Well actually' they say, 'we don't know him at all.' Embarrassed silence. 'It's just that . . . well . . . er . . . he's the only *other* bird-watcher we've ever seen.' I have got beyond the reply that tries to prod their memories. I've even got beyond telling them that some well-known people, people whose names and faces are household words and television images, are bird-watchers.

'Spike Milligan? Billy Fury? Oh . . . no . . . not that nice man that reads the news . . . him too? Oh no.' I got beyond that stage by feeling somehow that it was a rather peculiar illness, something perhaps that should not be mentioned in polite conversation, even if television personalities did do it.

Another tack is equally inclined to make one feel slightly guilty or unclean about the business.

'Oh . . . you're a bird-watcher' . . . A delicate bending of the body and with an air of extreme secrecy: 'Do tell me, I've always wanted to know—what do bird-watchers do?' What on earth can one answer to that?

'Well . . . we . . . er . . . look at birds.'

'You *look* (?) at birds?'

'Well . . . actually . . . we . . . sort of study them.'

'You study their what?'

'Well . . . their . . . er . . . courtship, mating and all that.'

'You study their mating?'

'Well . . . er . . . some of us do, most of us just look at birds and . . . er . . . er . . . enjoy doing it.'

'I see.'

Well, of course, they don't, they don't see at all. They are quite convinced that while bird-watching is good, clean, healthy fun for their ten-year-old boy, it most certainly isn't good clean fun for someone my age. Somehow, I say to myself, we have got to show people that bird-watchers can actually be ordinary, normal members of society, not strange, slightly juvenile boys that never grew up.

The trouble is that it's very difficult to say actually what a bird-watcher is, and what he does. Some for instance, do not like being called bird-watchers at all—they're ornithologists and join august bodies like the British Ornithologists' Union or the American Ornithologists' Union. A few bird-watchers manage to sneak into the unions without being noticed. Some do it to get the publications at half price, others because they like letters after their names: MBOU and AAOU look rather well. Yet others do it because they would like to be serious ornithologists, if only they had the time.

Of course, the unions do have a lot of non-bird-watchers as members, for there are serious ornithologists to be discovered here and there—mainly there, locked away in university common rooms. They are the people who write the papers that we read the summaries of. They are ornithologists and may well be bird-watchers as well—the same cannot be said for those who write papers whose summaries we do not bother with, or are completely unable to read. Titles like 'Depletion of adrenal ascorbic acid and cholesterol: a comparative study' and 'The role of intraocular pressure in the development of the chick eye' leave me a little cold. But then I suspect that other specialists in these areas might get very excited about such papers. They may conceivably completely change the direction their work had been taking.

Many more of our fellow bird-watchers are happiest in the field, watching and recording what they see—that is why the British Trust for Ornithology's Atlas Project was such a success. You didn't have to write up results and go through all the paraphernalia of publication, you didn't have to travel, or even be brilliant in the field of identification. You simply had to work your local area to death to find every breeding bird you could. It was like a gigantic competition with best totals published every season. No doubt the Atlas will turn out to be a very useful document indeed, but I have a sneaking feeling that perhaps it was almost, if not quite, as valuable to get so many people working so hard on their local birds. A lot of people got an awful lot of satisfaction from that.

These amateur scientists are, in the main, bird-watchers. They like to feel useful and not simply self-indulgent when they watch birds. The lesson of the Atlas is that bird-watching for most people is largely a matter of seeing what you can find—not of sitting for hours at a time watching a particular pair of birds, or even counting a few thousand ducks on an unromantic concrete-banked reservoir.

But not everyone wants to feel useful. Some are purely selfish, they want to watch birds because they want to watch birds. They may or may not keep records, and if they do they may or may not be published in local reports. They may be tick-hunters chasing rarity after rarity to add to their year or life list, or they may just enjoy the tits and other birds coming to their garden feeders. Quite a number apparently spend the winter reading bird-books beside the fire, the spring planning outings, the summer on holiday and the autumn gathering their winter books together.

Some bird-watchers I know join bird-protection organisations and get very involved in ensuring that the rest of us have some birds to watch in the future. Mind you, the more serious members of this group have an engaging habit of calling themselves 'conservationists' and getting themselves involved in 'ecology'.

So we have ornithologists (obscure and not so obscure), field-ornithologists, protectionists, conservationists, ecologists, not to mention ethologists, embryologists, parasitologists and simple ringers—all of whom may or may not be bird-watchers. Funny the way that most of us steer clear of 'bird-lover' as a term to describe ourselves!

Clearly we are not much nearer deciding what a bird-watcher is than when we started, but we have established a few guidelines and one very important rule. That is that no one activity picks out a bird-watcher as such; or put simply, you can do all sorts of things that count as bird-watching.

If then bird-watching is such a varied activity, it does seem strange that bird-watchers should be attacked by so many of their fellows for such a variety of heinous offences. Offences like betraying the sacred trust handed down by our ornitho-forebears by not sending in records to the appropriate authorities. Like chasing rare birds when one should be studying common ones. Like committing small birds to a life of shackles by lumbering them with numbered alloy rings round their legs. By trespassing to see birds that only the few have permission to see. By telling others where and when they can see birds and thus encouraging their enjoyment—nasty that. I have heard of some people who do not record which birds eat

49

their peanuts, and some that walk through the countryside without bothering to plot the transect that they are making. A particular group even photograph birds in the intimacy of their own little nests.

It is possible, but unnecessary, to argue each of these cases one by one and take the rest of this article to do so. But only one point need be made. We are all different and all enjoy birds in different ways. Provided that the birds come to no harm we should be tolerant of what others get from their own methods of watching birds.

The most widely attacked group of all are the tick-hunters or twitchers. I have written a plea for the twitcher elsewhere and here simply ask for the same tolerance that each of us expects for our own pursuits for those that like knocking up big lists. In America twitchers are called listers, though there is one big difference—everyone who is not an ornithologist does it over there. Perhaps the Americans are just more open and honest about their sporting interest in listing than we are, for I have always had a feeling that most of us enjoy seeing a new bird once in a while.

In the States the American Birding Association (ABA) is composed of those who go birding: to all intents and purposes that means listing. There are articles on identification, on bird finding, on tours and field trips and periodic analyses to see who is doing best. Peter Alden, for instance, sees over 2,000 species per annum and in 1973 went over the 4,000 life mark. That same year Stuart Keith (actually British) went over half the world's birds seen and identified, that's 4,325 plus. Why, I wonder, is listing or twitching so serious over there and so frowned upon here? Of course, it isn't just openness and honesty, there are more serious elements at work. The Americans lack the traditions of amateur fieldwork that gave rise to the BTO. Instead they have inherited the tradition of frontiers to be explored and so there is plenty of valuable bird-spotting still to be done. Ornithology was part of the curriculum of universities long before it became respectable over here, providing an opportunity for the more enthusiastic to obtain an academic training rather than join in amateur research. But perhaps the most important factor of all is the geography, having a continent to explore with the chance of picking up something in excess of 500 regular species, rather than an offshore island where a large part of the total list is made up of vagrants and accidentals. An American who wants a new bird can hop in a car and be back having seen it breeding within the country's borders within a couple of days. A Briton of any experience would find it easier to chase a vagrant. Listing may be more acceptable because of the frontiersmanship quality of the American personality and because every record is significant. In Britain another Radde's Warbler more or less makes little difference—except, of course, to the individual.

But tickers are not by any means the only group that are attacked. Many bird-watchers are downright derogatory about those who just feed garden birds. In fact in many people's terms they do not even count as bird-watchers. I've always found such attitudes rather strange, particularly among those who are themselves members of a highly attacked group.

Even the basic bird-watcher, a unique concept if ever there was one, is not immune from criticism. To the scientist, Mr Basic Bird-Watcher wastes his time when he could be better employed. The protectionist-conservationist seeks his support but also criticises his lack of active involvement in the cause. The twitcher simply refers to Mr B. B-W as a 'dude'—a term that lumps all non-twitchers, whether they are interested in birds or not, into one large conglomerate. But Mr B. B-W is the backbone of all of our activities.

Who is he? What does he do? Perhaps the answer to these

questions may help us to understand what bird-watching is really all about.

Mr B. B-W was a bird-watcher as a boy. His parents encouraged his interest and bought him a pair of binoculars and he spent the hours of summer wandering the surrounding countryside—for like most bird-watchers he lived in a town. While his parents became rather worried at his continuing enthusiasm at the age of sixteen, he had now joined the local natural history society and was spending more time travelling with the club to see birds. His life-list, neatly ticked off in his field guide, had by now grown to over 230 and he had heard of Cley-next-the-Sea. He was also working on migrants at the local reservoir and taking part in several of the BTO investigations. He was a trainee ringer and had enjoyed a few weekends at bird observatories. He has now reached the crisis point in his career; he may easily decide that bird-observatories are the only sensible places to live, or he may become a twitcher. He may pursue A-level zoology with the ambition of university and an academic career in birds. But most likely he will find a girl friend, get married, get a mortgage and abandon birds. A warning to unmarried young ladies—this is a temporary pause.

After a few months or years he will be out bird-watching again, involved in the natural history society and spending his weekends on field trips. It's a compromise. He devotes some of his life to his family and some to his hobby—both suffer but both are maintained. He thus becomes Mr B. B-W, keen on BTO work but not too active, a member of the RSPB, going bird-watching alternate weekends, some with the club, spending a few pounds a year on books and magazines and enjoying a summer holiday that is a mixture of birds and buckets-and-spades.

That's Mr B. B-W. The fate of birds in Britain is in his hands.

Page 53 (*above*) A flock of migrating duck, mainly Teal; (*below*) Tufted Duck

Page 54 (*above*) Duck's eye view of Nacton decoy pipe; (*below*)
Sparrowhawk at plucking post

I am often told that bird-watchers are mean—in that lies their downfall. Mr B. B-W does not contribute. He pays a couple of pounds to his club, a few to the BTO/RSPB, buys a few books and that's that. Total cost £20 per annum—perhaps less. Compare that with amounts spent by other users of the countryside—dinghy sailors, water-skiers, shooters, fishermen and, of course, golfers. Will Mr B. B-W pay to watch birds in the same way as others pay to enjoy their hobby? The answer is 'No'. Perhaps one day, in the not too distant future, birds will be so scarce that he will have to pay. But then the very vagrants that excite most of us are unlikely to be confined to the reserves and refuges of enterprising wildlife societies.

Bird-watchers are generally part-time enthusiasts not willing to pay much to enjoy their hobby. They are as variable as are people themselves and they don't all wear tweeds and deerstalkers. They are active and inactive, but above everything else they share a common interest. That's why it seems so strange that they should be attacked by their fellows. A little tolerance within and a concerted drive to ensure that birdwatching becomes ever more contagious is needed. Otherwise, one day, we shall all have to pay to watch birds. Mr B. B-W beware.

Where do all our ducks come from?

Jeffery Harrison

Where do all our ducks come from? This is no mere academic question; it is one with vital implications for conservationists, among the ranks of whom must now be numbered wildfowlers, who in the past twenty years have come to appreciate more and more that their quarry species do not fall like manna from heaven, year after year, out of an apparently boundless Arctic. Indeed there can be few true wildfowlers any longer in western Europe who do not appreciate that migratory wildfowl are an international responsibility. There is a 'harvestable surplus' which can safely be culled each year, but it is also recognised that this surplus varies year by year according to the breeding season. In the north-west European 'flyway' at least, the duck population is sufficiently well monitored to give advanced warning of trouble, so that any shooting of a quarry species would be stopped if a serious decline were demonstrated. This has happened already in the case of the Brent Goose, which is now protected throughout its entire range, following the alarming decline after a parasitic disease had devastated its main winter food supply of eel-grass in the 1930s.

The organisation responsible for the collection and interpretation of all the data from Europe and North Africa is the International Waterfowl Research Bureau (IWRB), whose headquarters are at present with the Wildfowl Trust at Slimbridge, where Professor Geoffrey Matthews is fulfilling an international role as its Honorary Director.

Eight Flyways

Ringing results and field observations have shown that there are at least eight flyways originating in northern Eurasia, which may, for administrative convenience and with a good deal of biological foundation, be defined as the north-west European flyway (our own from west Siberia to the British Isles); west Siberia–Mediterranean–North Africa; central Siberia–Caspian–East Africa; central Siberia–Indian sub-continent; eastern Siberia–Burma; eastern Siberia–China; far-eastern Siberia–Japan; north-eastern Siberia–North America. From this, it is obvious that the massive territories of the Soviet Union play a vital role in the future well-being of this great Eurasian wildfowl population and it is therefore most encouraging that the Soviet Union has played a major role in the activities of the IWRB since 1966.

Situated as they are, a group of temperate islands in the Atlantic off the south-west European mainland, the British Isles provide vital wintering grounds for wildfowl of the north-west European flyway and become even more important when spells of severe weather extend to the Low Countries. At this time, particularly when the shallow Ijsselmeer and the new polders of the former Zuider Zee in Holland become icebound, great numbers of duck, including such characteristic hard weather species as Smew, move across the North Sea.

American Duck

However, the British Isles also provide winter quarters for

large numbers of wildfowl on the Greenland–Iceland flyway. So far as duck are concerned, probably very few come from Greenland, but large numbers come from Iceland, mainly to Ireland and Scotland, although a Scaup ringed on Lake Mývatn has been recovered in the extreme south-east in Kent. This is a regular migration route, but other duck species do accidentally reach these islands from the North American mainland. Some are almost annual drift migrants, carried across the Atlantic during the autumnal westerly hurricane season which originates on the eastern American seaboard and coincides with the duck migration to the southern USA and Mexico.

A final flyway comes from North and West Africa (especially Senegal), which brings our only duck summer visitor, the Garganey. One rarity, the Ruddy Shelduck, also undoubtedly occasionally reached the British Isles as a genuine straggler from the Mediterranean, particularly in the two invasion summers of 1886 and 1892, long before they were commonly kept in captivity.

Although escapes from captivity no doubt confuse the situation, two species are probably reaching this country from central or southern Europe. The Red-crested Pochard appears to be increasing its numbers particularly in Switzerland, and is now breeding regularly in Holland. Over the past twenty years it has been recorded more frequently in Britain, especially in the south-east, while one ringed in Essex was later recovered in Holland. There have been two breeding records—in Lincoln in 1937 and in Essex in 1958. Both were thought to be by feral birds. Be that as it may, the Red-crested Pochard would make a magnificent addition to our commoner waterfowl and it is to be hoped that its spread will continue.

The ferruginous Duck breeds locally in central and southern Europe. The number of British sightings have increased since World War II, the majority coming from eastern England in winter. No doubt, the greatly increased number of bird-watchers accounts for part of this increase.

Feral Breeders

Three species recently accepted onto the British 'list' originated from captive stock. They are the North American Ruddy Duck, Mandarin and Egyptian Goose.

The Ruddy Duck, which originated from the Wildfowl Trust, now breeds regularly in the wild in both Gloucestershire and Somerset and has bred as far away as Hertfordshire and Staffordshire, while the first individual was reported from Kent in 1971. It is susceptible to severe weather, but the mild weather of the past eleven years has aided its spread.

The Mandarin, a spectacular native of eastern Asia, has established itself in Britain during the past fifty years, mainly in Surrey, Berkshire, Bedfordshire and Perthshire. At times, in winter, particularly at Virginia Water, it has been seen in flocks numbering over a hundred. As a member of the 'perching duck' it tends to favour wooded pools and so occupies an ecological niche in which it does no harm to other species.

The third species to have originated from captive stock dates back to the eighteenth century and is the aggressive Egyptian Goose which is in fact a duck, with little to recommend it. Fortunately it has not been particularly successful and it is regularly breeding only in north and east Norfolk. It may be slowly spreading, however, for a pair tried unsuccessfully to breed in Kent in 1972.

This general picture of where our ducks come from is not complete without mention of the home-bred duck, for a certain number do originate from these islands. By far the commonest is the Mallard. Other species are in much smaller numbers. Atkinson-Willes and Yarker have estimated 12,000 pairs of Shelduck, 2,000 pairs of Tufted Duck (excluding Ireland), a maximum of 1,000 pairs of Shoveler, 350 pairs of Wigeon and 200 pairs of Pochard.

Duck Factory

None of these figures apart from the Shelduck are of international significance, and the unfortunate fact is that whereas our temperate Atlantic climate is of great value to wintering duck, it is very often unfavourable for breeding in comparison with the hotter continental climate of the great Baltic–West Russian 'duck factory' area, where most of our winter immigrants are hatched.

This is well demonstrated in WAGBI's duck production survey, based on a wing analysis of duck in the bag. In September–October 1972 there were 39 per cent young Mallard in the bag in Kent, which increased to 64 per cent for the sample from November to the end of the season, due to overseas arrivals.

Some duck originate as hand-reared birds, liberated on to reserves. In the past nineteen years WAGBI has released over 175,000 Mallard in this way, all carrying rings. Their survival and mortality rates have shown conclusively that these duck have played a significant part in the increase of Mallard in the British Isles during this time.

The Gadwall is another bird which has been considerably increased by introductions. Probably the entire East Anglian population originates from birds released by Lord Walsingham in the 1850s. More recently WAGBI hand-reared Gadwall of East Anglian stock have been established in West Kent and are probably very slowly increasing. Ringing recoveries have shown these birds to be migrants to the French coasts of the Bay of Biscay in winter.

This, then, is the overall picture of where our duck come

from. It is now necessary to examine the two main flyways in more detail.

Baltic Flyway

It was encouraging to learn from Professor Isakov of Moscow that the only area where wildfowl have not decreased in the USSR is that containing the West Siberian–Baltic–North Sea population, which has in fact probably shown some increase. This is the only area which is adequately covered by a chain of wildfowl refuges, of which Great Britain provides no less than forty-one National or Regional Wildfowl Refuges plus a much larger number of local reserves. This north-west European flyway is also the only one which is adequately monitored.

The five common dabbling duck which visit the British Isles on the North-west European flyway—Mallard, Teal, Wigeon, Pintail and Shoveler—all nest around the Baltic, with the lakes east of Leningrad the most important area of all. The Mallard has the most westerly breeding range of the five, extending from the Channel coast of France, north to the Arctic Ocean in Swedish and Norwegian Lapland and south-westward through Finland to the foothills of the Urals, north of the Caspian Sea.

In contrast, the breeding range of our Wigeon lies furthest to the east, extending from northern Scandinavia and Finland, north-eastwards almost to the Taimyr Peninsula and southwards through central Russia to the north Caspian and the Sea of Azov. The eastern limits of the Teal's breeding range runs along the coast of the Barents Sea, just to the east of the northern end of the Urals and thence southwards to the western shore of the Black Sea and covers the remainder of north-west Europe, but it is only sparsely distributed in Scandinavia, Denmark, Germany and Holland.

Our Pintail breed in northern Scandinavia, Finland and north-west Russia, eastwards to the Kara Sea and southwards beyond the Urals, thence westwards through central Russia to the Latvian SSR. The Shoveler is even more limited with its range, not reaching the coast of the Barents Sea or extending east of the Urals.

Duck from Boxes

The three common diving duck of this flyway are the Goldeneye, Tufted Duck and Pochard. The former nests in the forest zone in Sweden and Finland around the Gulf of Bothnia. It is probably true to say that a large proportion of our wintering Goldeneye have hatched inside nesting boxes put up specially for them. It must also be remembered that any change from forestry in this area could have a serious effect on the British Goldeneye population.

The majority of our wintering Tufted Duck breed from the Baltic eastwards through north-west Russia to the Gulf of Ob in western Siberia, beyond the Urals. Pochard extend as far to the east, but with a more southerly range through central Russia and reaching westwards into northern Germany. There is considerable overlap in the Baltic area and the lakes north of Moscow, which is the most likely area for hybridisation between these two species, which is now known to occur quite frequently in the wild. Pochard ringed as young in south Germany and Czechoslovakia have also been recovered in Britain and the furthest ringing recovery is from the Sea of Oklotsk, 4,500 miles to the east.

A number of other species of duck use this flyway. Ringed Gadwell have been reported from Germany and Poland, Common and Velvet Scoter from Finland and Goosanders from Sweden, Finland and north-west Russia.

A great deal more information remains to be gathered for both the Scoters, Scaup, Long-tailed Duck, Red-breasted Merganser and Smew, all of which use this flyway in numbers, but as yet their exact breeding range has still to be defined. So far as is known, no Eiders reach Britain from the Baltic, but those in south-east England are known from ringing to be associated with the Danish and Dutch population on the Friesian Islands.

One rarity from the Arctic Ocean is Steller's Eider, which has now been identified in this country on eight occasions—six in Scotland. These are vagrants and one lost drake has been present in the Outer Hebrides for eighteen months and has attempted to hybridise with Common Eiders.

One other rarity which breeds in central and eastern Siberia should surely be given official recognition as a 'British' bird and that is the Baikal Teal, which has now occurred three times in Scotland (Fair Isle 1954; Elgin 1958 and Caerlaverock 1973) and once in Ireland. It is a migratory species to the Far East, but is more likely to appear as a vagrant than the non-migratory Steller's Eider.

Moult Migration

Shelduck, which nest in Britain, undertake a 'moult migration' in late summer to the remote sandbanks—the *Knechtsand* —in the Heligoland Bight, where they are joined by others from the north-west European coast and the Baltic. Later they are joined by the young and those adults which remained behind to care for the nurseries. These sandbanks provide a safe area to pass their flightless period, for unlike many other species of duck, the Shelduck's eclipse plumage does not become cryptic while it is flightless.

Recently a plan was proposed by the West Germans to

reclaim the *Knechtsand* for amenity. Fortunately prompt action by the International Waterfowl Research Bureau and West German conservationists was able to prevent this happening. Curiously, one group of about a thousand Shelduck remain in Britain to moult on Bridgwater Bay. The others return to Britain from mid-October onwards depending on the severity of the weather and the peak population is seldom recorded before Christmas.

As to the actual factors controlling duck migration on this flyway, there remains a great deal of mystery. In general, the autumn migration seems to take place in a series of comparatively small journeys in a south-westerly direction ahead of hard weather.

In recent years a mid-summer influx of various duck from north-west Europe has been recorded in south-east England, mainly drakes. This includes up to 3,000 Pochard on Abberton reservoir in July, while arrivals of Pintail, Wigeon, Teal, Garganey, Shoveler and Scaup have been recorded in inland Kent and London. It is possible that this is part of a 'moult migration'.

The next wave of duck moves into eastern England in August and September, again with a high proportion of adult drakes. This is often followed by a lull in October and further increases in November and December. By the end of the year, the duck population appears to be distributed throughout its normal winter quarters in western Europe. What happens in the New Year very largely depends upon the severity of the weather.

Traditional Wintering Grounds

Many duck no doubt have traditional winter quarters to which they return each year. A wonderful example of this was a Teal which the late General Wainwright caught in six consecutive winters at Abberton. Not only did it return to the same reservoir, he caught it in the same trap! A hybrid Pochard × Tufted Duck was also identified on the same water in west Kent in two consecutive winters.

It must not be assumed from this that duck have a rigidly fixed movement pattern. The establishment of new traditions plays an important role in their survival and few other groups of birds can be so adaptable.

Teal posed an interesting problem in this respect during the 1960s. Those which visit the British Isles appear to have a fairly narrow flyway from the Baltic through the Low Countries to reach our shores. In severe weather they may move on to France and the Iberian Peninsula or concentrate in Ireland. In spring they return by the same route.

Another population, immediately to the west, moves down from western Russia direct to the south of France, moving east in the New Year to Italy and Albania, thence northwards through Central Europe back to the Russian breeding grounds. The occasional Camargue-ringed Teal in Britain proved that there is some interchange.

For five winters from 1963 to 1967 Teal on the British flyway showed a dramatic fall in numbers. Curiously at this time, the percentage of young in the bag as revealed by WAGBI's duck production survey was high, ranging between 60 and 70 per cent from 1965–6 to 1967–8. This suggested the possibility that there had been a migratory shift to the east and indeed numbers were slightly increased in the south of France. Unfortunately, just at this time, large-scale ringing had been discontinued in Holland.

However, in the past four years, our Teal population has increased back to average and this in spite of production figures ranging from only 50 to 65 per cent. The evidence for some kind of migratory shift seems strong and this demonstrates the need for the combined use of duck counts, large-scale ringing and production surveys, all on a long term basis.

Differential Migration

Some species of duck show a differential migration pattern particularly well. An excellent example is the Smew. On the Elbe the first to appear in November are all females and young. By January I found that the proportion of adult drakes there had risen to 88 per cent. By March it had fallen to 53 per cent. In contrast, in January on the Ijsselmeer in Holland I found that a flock of 1,800 Smews contained only 17 per cent of adult drakes. From this, it would seem that the adult drakes are better able to withstand hard weather than the females and young which move further south-west to warmer winter quarters. This is confirmed by the fact that male duck are known to have higher basal metabolic rates than females.

Differential migration is a natural phenomenon therefore, which tends to separate the sexes and the young of some duck in winter. It may be extended in times of abnormally severe weather as in the winter of 1962–3 when exceptional numbers of wildfowl moved into southern England from the Low Countries. It soon became obvious that the effect of the cold was more severe on ducks than drakes.

In an earlier, less severe spell in 1947, the Wigeon packs in Kent had split up, the ducks coming in to feed in the lee of the seawalls, whereas the drakes were strong enough to stay out on the more exposed saltings. In 1963 this went a stage further, for the ducks migrated away, so that the proportion of drakes in mid-February reached a peak of 75 per cent. Of the sexed casualties, 56 per cent were ducks. In Shelduck casualties, the proportion was even higher with 84 per cent ducks.

Onward Flight

It only remains to mention that a small proportion of duck on the north-west European flyway move on beyond the British Isles. Teal, as already mentioned, and Shoveler, may move to southern France and Iberia in hard weather, also the occasional Mallard. More recently it has been discovered that some of our Pintail move as far south as Senegal in West Africa.

The Greenland–Iceland flyway differs from the north-western European one in that the duck, as would be expected, concentrate mainly in Scotland and Ireland, and perforce they come direct across the North Atlantic. So far as is known, very few duck, in contrast to geese, come from Greenland. It is highly likely that the majority of the seventy or so King Eiders which have occurred in Britain originate from their most important moulting area in west Greenland, which consists of the Canadian and Greenland population, although possibly some would be from Spitsbergen or Arctic Russia.

The regular migratory duck of Icelandic origin are Gadwall, Teal, Wigeon, Tufted Duck and Scaup, probably Long-tailed Duck and Common Scoter. The few records of Harlequin Duck, involving eleven individuals in Scotland and northern England, will also almost certainly be from the nearest breeding grounds in Iceland.

One notable exception to this list is the Mallard, for both Greenland and Iceland birds are virtually sedentary, feeding in open water along rocky coasts in winter. The Greenland bird is a distinct race, with a heavily spotted breast shield, which obtains a great deal of its winter food by diving.

It is ironic that whereas the waters around Iceland are comparatively free of oil pollution, winter concentrations of diving duck in eastern Scotland, particularly in the Firths of

Forth and Tay are now in greater danger of major oiling calamities than ever before.

While there is no regular flyway from the North American mainland, it is probable that never a year goes by without some transatlantic drift migrants being recorded somewhere in the British Isles, with Scotland and Ireland by far the most likely places for them to be found, although no less than five species— American Wigeon, Green-winged Teal, Black Duck, Ring-necked Duck and Surf Scoter have occurred in the extreme south-east in Kent.

It is interesting to look at their comparative frequency of occurrence, the approximate numbers of each being as follows: Surf Scoter 100; American Wigeon 50; American Green-winged Teal 50; Blue-winged Teal 30; Ring-necked Duck 10; Bufflehead 5; Black Duck and Hooded Merganser 4 of each. These are obviously minimal figures for the females of most are easily overlooked or difficult to identify. It is surprising that the most frequent should be a really tough sea-duck like the Surf Scoter and one is tempted to wonder whether British waters may not be within its extreme normal range.

American Green-winged Teal have become virtually annual, no doubt largely due to increased bird-watching and greater knowledge of duck identification by wildfowlers. It is much easier to envisage this species being carried across the Atlantic on strong westerly winds than a Surf Scoter.

The most astonishing record of American Wigeon was a gathering of thirteen which assembled at Lough Akeragh in Co Kerry in October 1968, at a time when we were there and we actually witnessed the build up from the original four birds which we found. Later we were to see one of the others arrive, spiral down to the water and fall asleep exhausted, whereupon we walked almost up to it!

One of these was shot nearby in the same month and had been

ringed in New Brunswick, Canada. Another Canadian-ringed bird had been recovered in Shetland two years earlier and since then a Canadian-ringed Blue-winged Teal has been recovered in Suffolk.

What the ultimate fate is of these transatlantic vagrant duck remains unknown. Other than perhaps the Surf Scoters, they are undoubtedly lost and occasionally they reappear on the same water in subsequent winters. A drake Ring-necked Duck was seen in Co Armagh from 1960 to 1968, being joined in the last year by another which had been in Co Down in the previous two winters. Notable absentees as yet from the British list include Cinnamon Teal and Canvas-back.

Finally, this article does not consider in detail where our home-bred birds go to in winter, although the great majority are largely sedentary within the British Isles. To end on a rather lighter note, there is one astonishing record of a Mallard, caught, ringed and released in East Anglia by Professor Geoffrey Matthews as part of his orientation studies, which must have somewhat confused it, for it was later recovered in Alberta, Canada and experts are quite undecided as to which way round the world it went!

A bird of prey odyssey

Leslie Brown

In 1970, when I was living in Kenya, I was asked to write a main volume in the New Naturalist Series about British birds of prey. Rather foolishly I accepted, thinking that I would be able to extract from British journals and books, supplemented by continental European material where necessary, all that was known. In the autumn of 1970 I did a month's reading in the Edward Grey Library at Oxford, contacted the British Trust for Ornithology, Nature Conservancy, and the Royal Society for Protection of Birds, and found out just how wrong I was.

Unpublished Material

It was all too clear that what was printed in the literature, either in Britain or in Europe, was inadequate. There were several massive ongoing studies in preparation, one of twenty years' duration on the Welsh Red Kite, another collating and analysing more than twenty years' work on the Hen Harrier in Orkney, and others. I knew that the Loch Garten Osprey eyrie, for instance, had been watched day and night during the season for seventeen years, but that, apart from Philip Brown and George Waterston's early book *The Return of the Osprey*, the material had not been analysed. I knew that

Page 71 (*above*) Hobby which has taken over a crow's nest in Berkshire; (*below*) Honey Buzzard

Page 72 (*above*) Peregrine; (*below*) adult male Whitethroat

Douglas Weir and Nick Picoszi on Speyside were in the early stages of a four-year study of the Common Buzzard; that Ian Newton was getting some remarkable data about Sparrow-hawks in Dumfries; and that there were other people in Britain who knew about still rarer birds such as the Marsh Harrier and Honey Buzzard, but had not published much or any of what they knew.

It was evident that if I was to make any sort of decent job of it I would have to plan a much longer trip later on, when these studies had been published, or gone a stage further towards completion. During it, I would have to contact most or all of the naturalists working on birds of prey and pump them for unpublished information. I could, of course, have sat back and written a nice sketchy little book based on the published data; but saw no point in writing one that would be out of date in a few years. For instance, I should have had to say that virtually nothing had been written about the habits of the Red Kite in Wales, whereas I knew that a great deal was known and would shortly be written up. Rightly or wrongly, this seemed to me an absurdity and I thought I would try to do better.

Even with the longer journey, and personal contacts and further reading I doubted if I could, in limited time, make as thorough a survey of existing literature and data as I would have wished. I now know I haven't, though I have picked up most of the published information and much unpublished.

Grinding Slog

My travels took me from Devon to Orkney and East Anglia to Wales. I saw much of Britain that was new to me, and made many new friends whom I hope, sometimes rather against hope, that I shall keep. I had some good fun and learned much that was new to me. But I can't deny either that it was a hard grinding slog, sometimes including a whole day in the field with some expert, and then cooking my own dinner and sitting up late typing a revised draft to show him next morning before moving on. I have learned from long and bitter experience that, in many cases, if one sends a draft for criticism that's the last one hears of it until the recipient blasts one for misquoting him. I felt that as far as possible I had to hit the nail on the head and drive it right home, red hot from its maker, whenever I could.

I began by reading *British Birds* issues from 1970 back to 1940, with some earlier papers; the whole of *Bird Study*; the handbooks and the relevant volume of Bannerman's *British Birds*. I added comparative material from continental and sometimes African studies. This preliminary work made it clear that there were some extraordinary lacunae in the knowledge of some relatively common British birds of prey, such as the Merlin and the Hobby (see plate, p 71); neither gets more than a few brief notes in most volumes of *British Birds*, and for the Hobby one must go to the early writings of egg collectors (which nevertheless contain some priceless gems of euphemism, eg 'visiting' nests). The commoner Merlin is even less well known; and one must go back to 1921 to find a reasonable account of breeding in Britain. The best breeding biology studies of the Sparrowhawk were done by Owen long before World War II; and there is little actual published data on the food of any of the three commonest British species, the Kestrel, Common Buzzard, and Sparrowhawk, though the general facts are known, and there are titbits scattered through the literature. I would have needed a winter in Britain, with those long dark evenings, to sift much more than I have from what is published.

My Odyssey really started in Devon, where I studied Buzzards briefly myself when I was young. In the library of Exeter University there is a magnificent PhD thesis by Peter Dare on the Dartmoor Buzzards, the work done in 1953–55, just after myxomatosis, but not completely written up till 1961. In the interim I had met Peter when he was working on Quelea control in Africa, and he now studies Oystercatchers, which apparently menace the cockle fishing industry. Only those students of birds of prey who have really sweated it out in the field themselves can appreciate the detail and hard work contained in this thesis, which I count among the ten finest studies of any bird of prey I know, and which never has been published in any accessible form. I spent two days on it; and wished I could have spared a week. Better still, I would have liked to visit his study area and see how the Buzzards were faring nearly twenty years later. Someone should do it but I could not spare the time.

Brain-picking

Likewise, I had to cut out a visit to Cornwall or Dorset to try to study Montagu's Harriers. I had already decided that original research by me could make little contribution to the book because of the time factor, and there seemed to be no one with an exhaustive knowledge of Montagu's Harriers whose brains I could ruthlessly pick and whose work is unpublished. If I wrong anyone in this, I am sorry: he's hiding his light under a bushel. A year's intensive field work on Montagu's Harrier in Britain would not only greatly advance what we know of this scarce and apparently decreasing species, but would provide material for a better study of Montagu's Harrier than is published anywhere. So, again, go to it, someone. And, if you do it, publish the results in journals, and

75

don't leave it in a prolix PhD thesis in a university library, hard to get at.

From here I moved east to the British Trust for Ornithology at Tring, to extract migration and nest record card data; and to the RSPB library at Sandy, which is a good and pleasant place to work in, where one can have a walk in the evening after a hard day's grind on papers, and the librarian, Dorothy Rooke, is unusually sympathetic and helpful. Then, on to Minsmere and other places in East Anglia to look for and at Marsh Harriers. I spent some fascinating hours in a hide at Minsmere watching a bigamous cock feed his two sitting wives. Clever chap that I am, I thought I had discovered another nest, for the cock twice fed a third hen in the same place. However, Bert Axell stoutly denied that there was any nest there, and of course he was right. I'm not so sure he was right, however, when he said that watchers could not keep an eye on the harriers and at the same time record useful scientific data. I believe they could; and would like to see dawn to dark watches organised, say twice a week, through the breeding season. I think this would produce a better account of breeding biology than exists anywhere in the literature on Marsh Harriers in any language. So there's another idea for someone, perhaps from Norwich University.

The Minsmere Harriers

The Minsmere Marsh Harriers are now the only regular breeding pairs in Britain, those in Dorset, Norfolk, and elsewhere in Suffolk having faded out. The reason is not clear, but is probably not due to poor breeding success, which at Minsmere and elsewhere in Britain compared favourably with that in the Camargue where the Marsh Harrier is abundant. Excessive human disturbance is the most likely cause; but

Dr Norman Moore believed that pesticides have also played a large part. If so, we may possibly see some improvement as the use of the more noxious pesticides is brought under reasonable control. There is already evidence, based on those sensitive barometers the Peregrine and the Sparrowhawk, that the pesticides are having rather less adverse effect on birds of prey than ten years ago; human disturbance, however, is now much worse.

I took time off to visit Horsey and see my old friend John Buxton, and talk about why Marsh Harriers have stopped breeding there, in a much larger marsh than at Minsmere. I actually saw not less than three Marsh Harriers there which, with the four at Minsmere, was probably half or more of the whole British population. As anyone who lived through the spring of 1972 will testify, it was generally cold and wet, and when in my van I was neither warm nor dry for weeks on end. However, on the one day's holiday I allowed myself at Horsey I was vouchsafed a golden day of May sunshine, in which I enjoyed to the full one of my rarest and keenest pleasures, a day on a dry fly trout stream. John told me that guests were allowed to catch three fish, but he did not believe that I would. I duly caught my limit, including the heaviest fish weighing $1\frac{1}{4}$ pounds, a big one for that river. It was a day to remember always.

Then, a swift run north to contact Ian Newton in Dumfries and see his Sparrowhawks (see plate, p 54). Small accipiters are not a speciality of mine; but my eyes were opened in two days with him. Ian knows his stuff thoroughly and, what's more, puts it on paper for others to read as soon as he can, thus making the work of the scribe much easier. We had good days in the field and chewed the fat to some purpose on other species as well; and as he also had all the BTO nest record cards on the Merlin I was able to extract necessary data from them too.

77

Egg Collectors

I had been to the Kite country in 1970, and had visited it again in April 1972, on my way south before my main journey began at Exeter. In 1970 I had learned of the twenty-year, unpublished study done by the Nature Conservancy and RSPB; and by 1972 this had reached the first draft stage. I was very kindly given access to it, extracted the meat, and wrote a draft chapter later for the experts to criticise. The two people who know most about Kites are Peter Davis of Tregaron Bog, and Peter Walters Davies. Peter Davis took me around, but in 1972 was down in the dumps because at least four Kite nests had been robbed by egg collectors. The man was caught and fined £100. However, this single individual probably frustrated the long-cherished aim of rearing twenty young Kites in a year. Even as it was, 1972 was a record year, with twenty-six pairs, twenty-two breeding, and, thanks to one pair which re-laid after being robbed, producing nineteen young. I saw seven Kites, probably about 10 per cent of the whole population, and felt that if left alone the Kite would spread, first to other suitable country in Wales, and later to Hereford, Devon and Somerset (where it is rumoured they have already tried to breed). Later, they could be reintroduced, via Buzzard foster parents, to other areas.

From Edinburgh north to Speyside to talk with Douglas Weir about Buzzards, Eagles, Peregrines, and Merlins, and to look at the RSPB Osprey record books to see if I could, in any reasonable time, extract good data from them. When I saw them I blenched; it would clearly take someone with an iced towel round his head about three months of eye-bugging research to extract the needed data. I reflected sadly that the RSPB had lost a magnificent chance of doing an extremely detailed research study at the Loch Garten eyrie, aided, as they have been, by an army of enthusiastic and often capable volunteer watchers. The Ospreys of Loch Garten have been watched more continuously and for longer than any bird of prey anywhere, and probably longer than any bird. Yet the records, which have been carefully kept every few minutes, are an amorphous mass, certainly omitting needed data but laboriously recording much that is unimportant, never summarised from day to day, week to week, season to season, or year to year. A golden chance thrown away.

The argument about what species of fish Ospreys take and how many, relative to the total fish population, is obviously a crucial one in conservation of a bird which was exterminated because it ate trout, and will be 'hammered' again if and when it becomes much more numerous, unless the attitudes of landowners change. I could only spare time to do a quick analysis of one year's results myself, already partly summarised. From this it was clear that the RSPB could do likewise, and do it better. Spin off from my gyrations in this part of the world has, I am glad to say, included a study of Osprey food and other data from the record books. Alas, the results of this will appear too late for my own book, as will Douglas Weir's paper on the Buzzard. One tries, but one can't always win.

The Eyrie of 1945

After beloved and well-known Speyside where, in 1946, I did the first of several detailed area surveys of Golden Eagles I moved north to Sutherland, where I did my last, in 1967. Before leaving I revisited an eyrie that I had not seen since 1945, to find in it an eaglet, a grouse, a hare, and a drake Mallard, recognisable by his bright orange webbed feet. The eaglet was one of two I had seen that year, the other being in a pine tree eyrie not used for many years if ever before. At present, in central and eastern Scotland, the Golden Eagle is on its way down and out. At least ten pairs, regular breeders in 1960, have now given up altogether or become irregular. The reason is, first and foremost, continual illegal persecution by gamekeepers despite the law. We know of pairs that often try but never succeed, in areas of abundant food supply. Recently, intense human disturbance in this and other popular mountain areas of Scotland has made it impossible for many pairs to breed. The offenders are casual walkers, bird photographers, and rock climbers, possibly in that order of importance. The Cairngorm Chairlift has put paid to one formerly very regular and unmolested pair, and others of long standing, now gone or irregular, are near the direct route to Ben Mac-Dhui and other high tops from Braemar. Gamekeepers and their employers are about as hopeless a proposition in 1972 as they were in 1872 without more vigorous legal measures against them, but one feels that rock climbers and others might at least be asked to keep out of certain areas, and that some of the thirty or so breeding pairs that fail each year from casual human interference might thus be saved.

North-west Sutherland, where I did my last survey in 1967, is another matter. Here there are few major peaks, and there are tracts where the foot of the tourist and rock climber, even the fisherman, never treads. Gamekeepers are interested in deer and salmon, not in grouse, and so they are indifferent to, or actively protect the eagle. I like, when I can, to add a little titbit of knowledge each time I visit an eagle area in Scotland, and this time I decided to visit a marginal breeding territory, occupied in 1967 by a sub-adult female. This subadult had one small nest, and was beginning another, but her range was overlooked by a well established pair on the other side of a valley. In 1967 an elderly shepherd had watched me climbing about on the cliffs (the only man who did, as far as

I know) and wondered what I was at till we had a talk. Now, grown older, he had left his isolated home, and I camped beside it in my van and wished I could buy it, for it is in idyllic surroundings, with the well established eyrie in view from the sitting room window. Probably it will first leak, then moulder, and finally be torn down by vandals unless the unlikely event occurs of finding another, younger man who does not want to watch the telly every evening.

As suspected, I found this marginal territory deserted. I saw no eagles, and the single small nest had mouldered into the ground and grown a crop of rushes. The other eyrie, occupied in 1967, was apparently empty this year. I could not spare three days to comb the whole area with a fine tooth comb, as is necessary actually to prove non-breeding. However, I felt certain that I was right, and that this was not a regular breeding site, but one only used from time to time when the better-established pairs all round permitted it, perhaps in years of exceptional food supply.

Orkney Highlight

I took in one or two other eyries I knew—all unoccupied— and then left Sutherland bound for Orkney, where I had not been since 1937. The old *St Ola*, travelling between Thurso and Stromness, used to go through Scapa Flow, but after a long career she has been replaced by a new boat which goes round under the splendid bird cliffs of Hoy. The mighty 1,000 foot cliff of St John's Head where, lying on my belly in 1937 I saw a slug-like creature among the rocks at the bottom and realised I was looking at an otter, has been climbed by experts with plenty of ironmongery since, as has the 400 foot Old Man of Hoy. I could see the areas here where I photographed Great Skuas and Great Black-backed Gulls, and two skuas now followed the boat, harrying the gulls that picked up scraps. Landing in Stromness, I was unable to locate the telephone box inside which three of us spent an excruciatingly cold night, jammed tight together, having been unable to find a bed anywhere. We had been viewed at intervals by a policeman, who never tried to find out what we were doing or invited us to the cells, which would have been welcome.

In Orkney I spent three days with Eddie Balfour and his Hen Harriers. For me, it was the highlight of the whole journey, for not only were the birds little known to me, but Eddie is unique. I know of no one working on birds of prey in the field who had attained closer rapport with the objects of his study. He left school at 14, but keeps meticulous records going back twenty-five years, which would put many professional ornithologists to shame, and from which he can check any point—such as whether a genuine clutch of two has ever been laid by a Hen Harrier. His records indicate that all such clutches originally were three or more, reduced by some mishap. To go out with him is an education. One sets out to visit a pair he has not seen this year. A man of rather few words he says, at the appropriate point, 'I chust want to check on this place.' We walk over a featureless expanse of Orkney moor and, on reaching a rushy depression much like any other he observes, 'she should pe chust apout here,' claps his hands and up she gets like a good girl. Or, if she does not, we look around, and within fifty square yards or so find this year's nest, deserted or empty through some mishap. His studies are not only the finest done of any Harrier species anywhere, but are also among the ten finest long-term studies of any bird of prey in the world. Now that he has retired from his duties as RSPB representative it is to be hoped that he will be given the funds and help to put a few coping stones on an already monumental volume of work.

From Orkney, swiftly back south, via Morvern and a few other places to Tring, where I actually wrote most of the book in Chris Mead's house. To get as much as possible done before leaving for Kenya I hammered the typewriter from seven to seven most days, and was dead beat at the end of each day. I felt I must complete all the chapters on individual species, and some others, before leaving for Kenya, where I could do the rest. Chris Salmon of the BTO nobly kept pace with my output, and all but a few of the experts to whom I sent revised chapters for review came up with useful criticisms. Those that did not have, of course, blasted me already for misquoting them.

Honey Buzzards

I took time off to visit Colin Tubbs in the New Forest, to discuss the Buzzard and Hobby material, and in the vague hope that I might see a Honey Buzzard. I went down with Richard Fitter on the first really hot day of summer. We sat in shirt sleeves on a hilltop, talking of Buzzards and Hobbies, and seeing certainly two, possibly three separate Honey Buzzards (see plate, p 71). Two, in the air together, proclaimed their identity by performing their unique display, raising the wings vertically above the back several times. Knowing the laws of gravity one wonders how the Honey Buzzard manages to do this without losing any height, as it appears to succeed in doing.

The secrets of the numbers and whereabouts of Honey Buzzards have been jealously kept, and I believe that more may be known about the species in Britain than is available in the continental literature, which mostly depends on old Danish studies by Holstein. It is a sad comment upon British birds of prey, and on British ornithologists, that those who know do not tell because of the army of twitchers and listers who might thereby be attracted to certain areas to tick off Honey Buzzards. Bert Axell at Minsmere had already told me his worst headache was people trying to get into Minsmere by the back door when they had been refused permits because the reserve was already full for a certain day. And, if a Gyrfalcon or a Rough-legged Buzzard appears in winter nowadays it is likely to be harried continuously by a stream of watchers, who contribute little that is useful, but who antagonise farmers and others by leaving gates open and trampling crops. This intense interest does at least enable a fairly full record to be kept of rare vagrants, where they are, and how long they stay. But I could not help reflecting that the same amount of time, petrol and ornithologist-effort would produce far better results if it were applied, let's say, to the diurnal behaviour of a pair of Marsh Harriers, under control and supervision, and decently recorded on forms that could be put into a computer if no one can find the time to look at them and analyse them with insight.

Back in Africa I concluded that, even if it was likely to be more lucrative than it is, I would never again try to write anything like a new naturalist book on British birds unless I was based on a British institution and in the good old civil service phrase, 'enjoying regular emoluments'. There is too much unpublished data around which a person with limited time cannot dig up, and in Africa I cannot get at even the main British journals, let alone the more obscure local bird reports. So the result of my Odyssey won't be as good as I, or others, might like it to be, though I think it is fair and most of my expert referees have said so. For good or ill it's done, and though it was hard work I had some good times too, and learned a lot. Maybe those who read the result may think my Odyssey was not altogether in vain.

Down on the farm

J. J. Flegg

Since World War II technology has progressed at such a rate that the more cautious onlooker might query whether we have any understanding of the effects of the changes that we are making. Well to the fore in the crusade against unthinking haste are professional biologists, ecologists and the rapidly growing army of amateur natural history enthusiasts—those concerned with their 'environment' as defined biologically rather than politically. Their concern can be summed up by considering an oak tree: it took 300 years to mature, and would take 300 years to replace—but it can be felled, and its site covered in concrete, in a couple of days.

Farming Revolution

Where does farming stand—traditionally one of the ultra-conservative industries—in all this? A journey through any part of the country, other than that concerned with hill-farming, will quickly give the answer. Farming has modernised, even revolutionised, at an astonishing rate. 'Intensive' is the keyword, 'specialist production' the economically dictated rule. It is sobering to consider that the child of the 1940s held the combine harvester in the same light that today's child would regard the prospect of a personal interplanetary space-ship sitting in the garage.

To obtain the high yields that an increasing population, an increasing living standard and an increasing profit margin dictate, fields enlarge while hedgerows, scrub and spinneys vanish before the bulldozer. Other plants—often called 'weeds' —are not allowed to compete for computerised synthetic fertiliser applications. These fertilisers, together with modern drainage techniques, have allowed the conversion of much marginal land into 'more productive' cropping regimes. Once the crop is established, other animals—often called 'pests'— compete for a share of the productivity bounty at their peril. But we are moving so fast that we may be in danger of distorting the picture. Let us examine the various developmental stages more closely.

Remarkable DDT

The exigencies of the war produced a remarkable chemical called DDT for short. It was remarkable for its effectiveness in controlling insect vectors of disease in tropical war theatres, and in controlling the personal parasite problems of the troops. Moreover it was incredibly cheap to produce. It was also remarkably persistent—that is, it remained active as a pesticide for many months. The full impact of this persistence was not to become apparent for many years—not unnaturally, because nothing of the sort had been encountered before. If the material was not immediately toxic to creatures other than the insects at which it was aimed, who was to expect the subsequent problems of accumulation?

DDT can persist in the soil, virtually unchanged in potency, for many years. An advantage, surely, in pest control, but at what environmental cost? In many animals and birds, particularly predatory ones, prey containing sub-lethal does of DDT is eaten, the DDT being stored in the predators' body fat

86

relatively harmlessly. But let some time of stress—a cold winter or raising a family—cause that body fat to be metabolised, and toxic doses of DDT are released. A survey, conducted by Dr Derek Ratcliffe for the British Trust for Ornithology (BTO) in 1960 and 1962, coincided with the later phase of a dramatic decline in the normally stable population of the Peregrine Falcon (see plate, p 72). Subsequent research indicated that the decline began in 1956–7 in southern England, later spreading steadily northwards. Despite continuing arguments between chemists and ecologists, it has become widely accepted that responsibility for this population decline (by more than 50 per cent) can be laid at the door of toxic synthetic chemical residues. The mode of action of the persistent organochlorine compounds (of which DDT is one) is particularly insidious, resulting, it has been suggested, in egg-shell thinning, egg breakage, reduced brood size and success, and sometimes non-breeding.

Sophisticated Compounds

Other, more 'sophisticated', compounds were developed on the theme of persistence as a positive value. Materials like dieldrin, aldrin and heptachlor for dressing spring-sown cereals resulted in widespread deaths of seed-eaters like the Woodpigeon and Pheasant. While the landowner would perhaps not be too saddened at the loss of Woodpigeons, the loss of his Pheasants, raised and nurtured at some considerable cost, was a price too high to be borne, and all lobbies combined to produce a voluntary ban on the use of these materials in 1961. While it is heartening to be able to report, from the latest (1971) Peregrine census, evidence of increasing populations and breeding successes at last, the life-span of these chemicals is such that peak concentrations have not been

87

reached in the seas in which they arrive via our ditches, streams and rivers.

Despite the necessarily circumstantial nature of much of the evidence linking bird deaths and population declines with the various agrochemicals, new materials are now subjected to field as well as laboratory tests before release. While some aspects of the tests relevant to wildlife leave scope for improvement, at least there is an acceptance of the dangers inherent in the situation, and of the need to examine the performance and problems of new materials before release, rather than picking up the pieces after a disaster.

Bird Benefits

Though there are other pressures exerted on farmland birds, are there any benefits for the birds in modern farming techniques? What damage have the prairies developing in eastern England caused to bird populations? Can we accurately assess this damage? Clearly if all hedges, scrub and woodland are removed from a farm, that farm will be the poorer for it; but are the dispossessed birds necessarily fatalities or merely displaced? If displacement does occur, what are the distance and time scales involved? These questions are as yet unanswered—partly because of the natural elasticity of bird populations so far as both numbers and movement are concerned, and partly because the magnitude of the study necessary to resolve the problem has so far prevented all but superficial attacks on it.

As with pesticides, we must resort to circumstantial evidence and to the results of surveys for information. Surveys, while lacking the statistical refinement of the designed experiment, do have several valuable assets: they are carried out at a large number of sites, scattered all over the country,

Page 89   (*above*) Barn Owl and young at their nest in a barn; (*below*) male Satin Bowerbird displaying to female

Page 90 (*left*) Bullfinch
stripping buds; (*below*)
Bullfinch at nest with young

by amateur ornithologists who know the area well, and the time committal per site is greatly in excess of that possible for the professional researcher. It could well be argued that these assets outweigh the disadvantages of lack of precision.

Population Index

Largely as a result of the impact of the concern roused by naturalists and ecologists in the 1950s (besides the Voluntary Restrictions of 1961) the Nature Conservancy commissioned the BTO to undertake a Common Birds Census on a series of farmland sites. Since 1961 some hundreds of farms have been covered, all over Britain, and censuses of their breeding birds have been taken on a series of visits (usually ten or more per season) in a succession of years. From these population figures an index of population change from year to year can be calculated, reflecting for each species the nationwide performance. The census is now thirteen years old, and the figures produced are beginning to become revealing. But a word of caution is necessary: in particular, we are looking at a very small piece of time in a natural sense. It is quite possible that some of the seemingly violent fluctuations revealed are fairly insignificant compared with long-term cycles that have, as yet, not appeared.

For some species—the Partridge is a good example—the picture is rather gloomy. Dr Dick Potts of the Game Conservancy has linked this decline to changing patterns of cereal growing. The removal of hedges and the use of weedkillers have eliminated the wild food plants of many of the food insects necessary for the survival of young Partridges. The insects on the cereals themselves in most years are just not sufficient, and the young starve. The Whitethroat (see plate, p 72) is in an even worse plight. This migrant warbler, so cheerful in the hedgerow, left in normal numbers in autumn 1968 for its winter quarters in Africa. How few returned the following spring! A number of possible reasons for this disastrous drop were investigated (including anti-locust spraying in Africa) but it would appear that a climatic upset caused their food supply to fail in spring 1969, and birds could not fatten-up normally for the long northward journey over the Sahara and many perished on the way. Subsequent climatic conditions in Africa and an increasingly rapid extension of the southern Sahara—now having a marked and sad impact on the nomadic peoples of the Saheel zone—have so far prevented any real recovery.

Boom Species

For other species, the picture is reversed. Striking examples are the Stock Dove and the Reed Bunting. Both species are resident throughout the year, and probably suffered similarly during the hard winters of 1961–2 and 1962–3. In the recovery phase of this setback, they have just not stopped!

A quick inspection of the index charts over the last decade indicates that, of the forty-nine species for which figures are available, twenty-two have shown an overall tendency to stay level, oscillating about a norm, while twenty-one have increased over the period in general, and only six have markedly declined. We should not, however, regard this as a sign that down on the farm everything is rosy. We have just finished a decade of mild winters and it may be that this lack of natural restraining factors has allowed populations to expand far more than we would normally expect. Nor should we forget the few, but perhaps important few, species particularly threatened. The Partridge we have seen—but what of the Barn Owl? Accepted, even welcomed, by the farmer as part of the natural system of rodent control, but often thoughtlessly deprived of nesting sites when old barns (see plate, p 89) are replaced by new asbestos structures, or when hollow trees are removed, for tidiness' sake, from hedgerows.

It would probably be fair to place concern for the future on the word tidiness: removal of dead timber, clearance of scrub, infilling of ponds, removal of weeds by herbicides, trimming to excess of road verges and field hedges—all with that motive. Do we really need to risk so much for such a small addition to the profit margin? Do we, as a nation, care so little for our farming scenery?—surely not. The situation looks good: a little forethought and it may stay that way.

Bowerbirds

Hans Beste

One of the most fascinating families of birds are the bowerbirds of the Australian region. Seven true species are found in Australia together with a further species often referred to as a bowerbird, but which in reality is a catbird. Bowerbirds stand out among other birds due to their habits of building elaborate structures from sticks which they decorate in various ways. These structures, known as bowers, serve as focal points for the bird's courting and mating activities during the breeding season. Even during the 'off-season' male birds rarely wander far away from these playgrounds. Not all bowers are constructed in the same way, nor do they run to stereotypes for a particular species but rather, following a basic pattern for a bird, great variation from bower to bower is the rule rather than the exception.

Australian bowerbirds are best divided into two groups: one, the avenue builders, with six representatives, and a second group, which one might call elaborate structure builders, of which there is only one species in Australia. Other species of the latter group are found in New Guinea. The eighth bird species, which builds a playground is somewhere outside this group, and is variously called the Tooth-billed Bowerbird, or Tooth-billed Catbird (*Scenopoeetes dentirostris*). This bird makes a stage rather than a bower and, as other catbirds have no building habits, this species presents taxonomic problems, which have contributed to it being placed with both groups by different workers.

The avenue builders can be further divided into fawn-coloured birds of the *Chlamydera* group, which are very closely related, not only in plumage, but also in the type of bower they build, and into more colourful species.

Elaborate Bowers

Unfortunately, only one species of bowerbird found in Australia builds a really elaborate bower. This is the Golden Bowerbird, roughly thrush-size, which constructs a bower averaging 2 to 4 feet, but at times reaching 8 feet in height. The male Golden Bowerbird is also one of the most strikingly coloured birds in its family with plumage that is rich golden-yellow on the chest, abdomen, upper back and friar's cap, as well as a yellow-tinted tail. The lower back, wings and facial plumage are brown, giving a contrast, which is only surpassed by that of the Regent Bowerbird whose main colours are black and gold. Female and immature Golden Bowerbirds lack the yellow of the male, and are brown on the upper surface, with greyish throat, chest and abdomen. Males only develop full plumage with sexual maturity, and this is thought to take at least three to four years. However, a bower is at times held and defended by an immature coloured bird, as my wife and I found during our stay in north Queensland recently. One of these bowers was previously constructed by a fully coloured male, but was taken over by a young bird when the old male either died or left the area. As the Golden Bowerbird is only found on a few mountain tops above two thousand six hundred feet, from near Townsville in the south, to Mount Finnigan near Cooktown in the north, it is not very well known, except to serious ornithologists who will penetrate into the rainforest jungles where the bird makes its home.

95

Decorations

To construct a bower, the male selects two small saplings, a few feet apart, across which a hanging vine or fallen stick forms a bridge which serves as a perch. One sapling, often higher than the second, is called the primary wall, and is surrounded by the bird with hundreds of short broken-off sticks. The bird arranges these so as to form a cone-type structure, several feet in height. The second sapling is decorated similarly, but usually not to the same height as the first. Pale green lichen is finally draped over the structure but more so over the higher wall, and more in the vicinity of the perch. Decorating takes place as the nesting season approaches, but fresh pieces of lichen are added throughout the breeding season. The bridge is also covered with lichen.

The Golden Bowerbird then collects white flowers and pale-coloured fruit husks which it places on the display stick, usually closer to the larger wall. One bird near Cooktown decorated its bower with masses of magnificent white Dendrobium orchids which it collected from the mountain top not far above its bower. However, this is the only bower that was decorated in this manner to our knowledge. The Golden Bowerbird was only discovered in this area a couple of years ago and this extended the known range of the species quite considerably.

Enticement

Bowerbirds construct their bowers to attract females to their territory, and the male's display to a female takes place on or near it. The display of the Golden Bowerbird consists of little more than the bird pressing itself against a small tree, while perched side-on to the tree trunk. This is not often recognised as part of the display. A more obvious display is the bird's fluttering in the air, while facing a tree trunk or the foliage of smaller saplings. We witnessed this display many times, and did not recognise its significance at first, until we realised that fluttering was only performed when females were perched near the bower. This unusual behaviour is in marked contrast to ground displays, normally shown by the avenue-building bowerbirds.

The bower of the Golden Bowerbird is not difficult to find if one follows the song of the male bird, but the nest is usually well away from the playground and is much harder to locate. Only a handful of nests have ever been found, and most of these have been in a niche between the roots of a tree, 1 to 4 feet from the ground. The female blends in well with this type of habitat, and as it is rather gloomy in the rainforest, nests are only found by someone accidently walking up to the female and flushing her.

Just after daybreak is the best time to observe the Golden Bowerbird. It is most active during this time when it decorates and attends to its bower. For most of the remainder of the day the male makes the rounds of the several perches it uses near the bower. These may be branches of trees or vines hanging loosely from the forest canopy. Every now and then the bird leaves the bower area to fly to a nearby fruiting tree. With a berry in its bill it returns to one of its favourite feeding perches, or feeding tables, as they are more commonly known. Accumulations of berry stones beneath a branch usually serve as a sure sign of a bowerbird's perch. The Golden Bowerbird, like the other species of its family, is an outstanding mimic of bird calls, and a keen bird student soon learns what species of birds are to be found in the areas surrounding the bower, without actually seeing them if he listens closely to the bowerbird's song. We found the bird most vocal when strange males entered his territory. However, when the other bird came too close to the bower which we were observing, the resident male would chase the intruder until it had crossed a small mountain stream that served as territory boundary.

Satin Reflections

Of contrasting plumage, the male Satin Bowerbird (see plate, p 89) is bluish-black all over, with a plumage that reflects like shiny satin. Only the bill and legs are of a contrasting yellow, but it is the eye which is the most striking feature of this handsome bird. This is a beautiful pale mauve in the male. Juvenile and female birds are green-backed, with a pale yellow chest and abdomen, covered with a horizontal pattern of broken bars of a darker tone. The eyes are bluish and green birds are most attractive in their own way. Mature black males are outnumbered greatly by green birds, a good indication of slow maturing in this species. The Satin Bowerbird, an avenue-builder, clears a patch of ground 3 to 4 feet in diameter, which it covers with a layer of small sticks to a depth of an inch or two. Two parallel walls of twigs are then erected in the centre of the stage. These walls are about 4 inches apart, and 12 to 18 inches in length. Their thickness varies, but in an elaborate construction they are 2 inches thick. Hundreds of twigs are used for each wall, varying from only a few inches to 18 inches in length. A completed wall is from 9 inches to 1 foot in height, but several sticks jut out above this.

Blue Playthings

When the basic structure is completed, the bird starts to decorate the playground in front of one end of the bower. Anything blue that the bird can find will be collected and placed onto the stage. While we were working at a bower, far from human habitation, blue-coloured berries and mauve flowers were the main items used. However, yellow fruits and berries, bleached animal bones and skulls, as well as rainforest snail shells, cicada shells and yellow leaves, served as decorations. As the Satin Bowerbird is found from Northern Queensland, down the east coast of Australia into central Victoria, it often builds its bower near towns, and human-made articles often find their way into its territory. Thus blue-coloured bottle tops, pieces of blue plastic, or anything predominantly blue will be picked up by the bird and brought to the bower. When we shifted some blue Quondong berries, a native fruit, from the area in front of the avenue, and placed these in the bower, the bird soon landed on the ground from its perch above our hide, and with much vocal activity, tossed them out by flicking them over his head. He then picked the berries up again, and replaced them one by one in their correct place on the playground, just in front of the avenue entrance. Shifting some of the mauve flowers off the playground onto a close-by vine evoked a similar reaction from the bird. Obviously, there was a correct place for these also and the bird placed each one just in front of the right wall of the bower, exactly where we had shifted them from. This concern for correct placement of decorations shown by the Satin Bowerbird is demonstrated by other members of the family, and indicates a high placement on the ladder of evolution by these birds within the avian world.

Painting the Walls

A bower is never really considered finished, and fresh sticks are added constantly, while others may be taken out. We witnessed a Satin Bowerbird pull down a complete wall one day, but it soon rebuilt it. Each stick is placed into the playground with the bird grasping it in its bill, about half way, and tilting its head sideways, pushing it into the mat of sticks making up the platform until the new stick stands up vertically.

This might take considerable pushing, and the bird will often try several places along the wall before it has finally satisfied itself with the effort. A most peculiar habit found with avenue-builders is that of painting the sticks of the bower walls with the juice of squashed berries. After filling its bill with the mulch of berries, the bird paints each stick by passing them through the slightly open mandibles. Some workers report that the Satin Bowerbird uses charcoal for painting, something we have not observed so far.

The mating display of the Satin Bowerbird is a most fascinating affair, and starts with the female arriving at the bower, while the male sings from its perch in a tree above. The female has been attracted by his song. She enters the bower and stands motionless in the centre of the avenue between the walls. The male flies down onto the playground and starts to dance around her. Spreading wings and tail, he gyrates in circles with head held low. Uttering his grating call he struts, then leaps and rushes from one end of the playground to the other. For several minutes the bird dances in this fashion while circling the bower. As the excitement mounts he moves closer to the female, which hardly moves during this performance. As the dance reaches a climax, the male bird picks up decorations and presents these to the female. A flower, a berry, then a snail shell and another flower is shown to her. Suddenly the female leaves the bower, and hopping on to a low vine or branch she crouches down low, and with wings quivering, presents herself to the male. He then leaves the playground and mating takes place.

Lilac Cape

The best known of all the bowerbirds are the brown birds of the inland and more open type savannah woodlands. The

Spotted Bowerbird, the most handsome of the four Australian species, is basically fawn coloured with bold brown and rufous spotting on the upper surface. It has a magnificent lilac-coloured cape fanning out from the back of the neck, which becomes visible when erected during display. Only mature males and old females have this cape, but young birds look little different otherwise.

Spotted Bowerbirds are found from north-western Queensland, through inland New South Wales, to north-western Victoria, although only one bower is still known in that state. Ruthless shooting over the years has contributed to the decline of the species in Victoria. Offenders usually excuse themselves with the explanation that the bowerbirds do extensive damage to their fruit crops, which is most unlikely, due to the scarcity of the species in the area. Spotted Bowerbirds, and others of this group, often live close to human habitation, and are thus well known to country people.

Five Pounds of Nails

The Spotted Bowerbird builds an avenue of sticks, like the Satin Bowerbird, but the walls of its bower are two feet or more in length, and it is not uncommon to find several bowers, built by the same bird, within a few feet of each other. Some of these are from previous years, but the bird may build more than one during a season. Whereas the Satin Bowerbird prefers blue and yellow objects, birds of the *Chlamydera* group have a preference for white, green and red trophies. They are very partial towards silvery reflecting articles, usually man-made, and pieces of glass, nails, and silver coins are often found in their bowers. One Spotted Bowerbird that we observed for some time had at least 5 pounds of roofing nails on its playground, pilfered from a 44-gallon drum full of these, which stood at least a quarter of a mile away outside a farmer's barn. This particular bird had also collected a pale blue toy duck, which although of the wrong colour, nevertheless seemed to fascinate the bowerbird. It was continually playing with it, and when we tied it to a branch above the bower, the bird took great delight in pecking at it continuously, making the duck gyrate in circles.

The largest of the brown birds aptly named the Great Bowerbird has the largest collection of objects, and one bower in Queensland which was near a rubbish tip, was covered with pieces of green glass and bright red plastic articles. Hundreds of white pebbles and bleached shells covered the playground. This species is very similar to the Spotted Bowerbird, and the mating and courting displays of this whole group are very much the same as those of the Satin Bowerbird. A marked difference, however, is that the male presents its lilac neck feathers to the female by erecting the plumes sporadically, especially when his back is turned towards her.

Shiny Side Down

In contrast to the other bowerbirds, the Tooth-billed Bowerbird or Catbird, often just known as Toothbill, has a unique playground. This rather sombre coloured brown bird, found in elevated rainforests of north Queensland, clears an area often 6 feet in diameter or more around small saplings. It then covers this with freshly collected green leaves, of different lengths, and from several species of trees. Some of these may be over two feet in length and up to a hundred have been counted on a playground. Whereas other bowerbirds decorate their bowers with various objects and take great care in placing them, the Toothbill is most particular that every one of his leaves is placed upside-down on the playground.

Each leaf as it is brought to the stage is placed with the upper and invariably shiny side down. To test the bird's reaction, we turned the leaves on one stage right side up. The Toothbill had flown off as we approached and thus did not witness our interference. Settling into a hide nearby, we did not have to wait long for him to come back. At first he flew on to the singing perch a few feet behind, and just above the bower. For a while he sang in his peculiar croaking voice, as if nothing had happened. But all of a sudden the singing stopped and the bird hopped on to the stage. It then proceeded to turn each leaf the right way up, and after a couple of minutes had finished the job. We repeated this procedure several more times, each time with the same reaction from the Toothbill. As some leaves became dry and started to curl up, they were replaced by fresh ones.

The Tooth-billed Bowerbird is more often heard than seen in its gloomy habitat of dense rainforest. It does not like sunlight and moves back into the shade of overhanging foliage should light fall on its perch during the day. When famous film-maker Heinz Sielmann was in Australia several years ago, he coined a phrase, which more than anything else describes the Tooth-billed Bowerbird. He called it 'a bird of the shadows'.

Although the playgrounds of bowerbirds are always on the ground, their nests are not. The Tooth-billed builds its nest at least thirty feet up in thick foliage, or attached to a vine. Avenue builders rear their young in nests usually ten feet up or more and only the Golden Bowerbird nests close to the ground. All members of the bowerbird family are predominantly fruit eaters, and most of them have striking plumage in one way or another. Several of them are excellent mimics of other bird songs, but it is the skilful bower building and elaborate courtship display on the playground which makes the family one of the most interesting groups of birds in the world.

Nipped in the bud

Ian Newton

Bullfinches in Britain now remove buds from fruit trees on such a scale as to present a major problem to the fruit-growing industry. This is especially so in south-east England, but also locally in East Anglia and the Midlands. But the problem is not new, for these birds were classed as pests as long ago as the sixteenth century, when the substantial reward of one penny was offered for the head of 'everie Bulfynche or other Byrde that devoureth the blowthe of fruit'. Damage has increased enormously since 1945, however, following the increase and spread of Bullfinches outside woodland. Nowadays, in extreme cases, whole orchards of trees may be almost stripped of buds, and yield only a few pounds of fruit instead of several tons. In comparison, damage to buds by other bird-species is negligible, though that by House Sparrows can be severe around human habitation.

Only the small embryonic centres from flower buds are eaten (those parts otherwise destined to become fruit), and the outer scales are shelled off. Buds destroyed are not replaced by the tree in the same year, but most fruit varieties make good the loss in the following year through the development of ancillary buds. In some types of plums and gooseberries, however, there is no regeneration of fruiting points, so that damage is cumulative. Occasionally leaf buds are also eaten, making it impossible to train the tree to good shape, and thus permanently affecting its cropping potential.

Bud Stripping

A Bullfinch can strip buds in a remarkably systematic manner: alighting at the tip of a branch, it works towards the trunk taking every bud in turn. On reaching the older wood, which bears fewer buds, it flies out to the tip of another branch and repeats the process. In this way, it can remove buds at a rate of thirty or more per minute, and since Bullfinches often gather in flocks of twenty or more, they can soon devastate a large orchard. They usually enter from adjacent woods and hedgerows, and attack the nearest trees first. As the days go by, they penetrate farther, stripping every tree in turn. The amount of damage varies greatly from year to year, however, depending mainly on when the birds start eating buds; in some years they begin as early as November, in others not until March, but once begun, the attacks continue until blossoming is over, about mid-May.

As a rule, plum and pear trees are most vulnerable, with gooseberries and currants next, and apples and cherries least, though different varieties are preferred in different months. The usual sequence of preferences in Kent orchards through the year is shown in the table (see p 109), but in areas where other varieties are grown the sequence differs. And within any one type of fruit, certain varieties are always more vulnerable than others. Among pears, for example, the varieties 'Williams', 'Dr Jules' and 'Conference' are preferred; among plums the various gages, and among apples dessert varieties are generally preferred to cookers. But the least favoured varieties are spared only when the birds have a choice, otherwise they too are eaten. There are no consistent differences in appearance, size or texture between buds of favoured and avoided varieties, and the preferences are probably governed by differences in time of bud swell, nutritive content and palatibility. At least in mid-winter, the birds choose those buds which provide the most nutritious diet at the time, for feeding trials on captive birds showed that the favoured varieties were also those on which the birds could best maintain their weight. Various ornamental shrubs, such as Forsythia, are also attacked in spring, probably mainly because their early flowering requires early bud swell, so that their buds are always more advanced than those of native trees.

Ends of the Range

Over most of Europe and Asia, the Bullfinch is found at low density in coniferous and mixed forest, which was probably its ancestral habitat. Only at the two ends of the range, in Britain and Japan, is it found at high densities in deciduous woods and cultivated land, and only in these areas has it become a serious pest to the fruit grower.

The bird nests in shrubs and hedgerows. In most years in England the first clutches are laid in early May and the last in mid-July but, in years of low population or abundant food, eggs may be laid until mid-September, so the last young fledge in October. A brood normally consists of four to five nestlings and, although each pair would have time to raise three to four broods in a year, few do so because of heavy predation on the eggs and young. Near Oxford, only one-third of all the clutches started in woodland, and two-thirds of those in farmland, successfully produce young. The farmland nests are more successful because the chief predators, Jays and weasels, are less numerous than in woods. After breeding the adults undergo a complete moult lasting, in each individual, ten to twelve weeks; and at the same season the juveniles have a partial moult lasting seven to nine weeks. At this time Bullfinches

Page 107 (*above*) Mute Swan in flight; (*below*) a Whooper Swan
feeding among Mute Swans at Barton-on-Humber, contrasting the
pattern and shape of their beaks

Page 108 (*above*) A Bewick's Swan—the distribution of the black and yellow bill markings is different in every individual, thus making identification and long-term study comparatively easy; (*below*) The Wakes, the Selborne home of Gilbert White, now a museum; White's study is to the right of the climbing shrub

The sequence of bud-preferences shown by Bullfinches in Kent orchards

	Months of damage	Remarks
Apples	January–April	Damage rarely severe. The buds of some varieties, such as 'Lord Lambourn' and 'James Grieve', are eaten when dormant, but most varieties only at bud-burst or at the 'pink-cluster' stage. In general, dessert varieties preferred to 'cookers'.
Cherries	November–January	Only 'Morello' suffers severe damage in the dormant stage. Ovaries from sweet cherries are sometimes taken in spring, but damage is rarely severe.
Currants, red and white	December–March	Time of peak damage varies, but is often severe.
Currants, black	March–April	Usually attacked only after bud-burst, but often severely.
Gooseberries	November–February	Damage often severe. 'Leveller' one of most favoured varieties.
Pears	January–March	Damage to some varieties often so severe as to result in complete loss of crop. In years when bud-feeding begins early, favoured varieties may be attacked in November, but usually the birds soon switch to plums and return to pears in January. The varieties 'Conference', 'Williams' and 'Dr Jules' are most vulnerable, 'Comice' and 'Hardy' least.
Plums	November–February	Damage to some varieties is often so severe as to result in complete loss of crop. Various gages, especially 'Golden Gage', preferred above all others.

remain hidden and inconspicuous, but after moult they begin to move further afield and, until the following spring, are often seen in parties of five to six individuals. But the largest flock seen in an orchard consisted of fifty to sixty birds, and the largest in farmland exceeded 150.

It is not certain why Bullfinches have increased in England, but they now live in closer association with man and in more open places than formerly. They are common now in parks and gardens, both urban and suburban, to which only thirty years ago they were rare visitors. In fact, the spread from wooded to more open country, and the extra food available there, might have been a major factor promoting their increase. These changes have so far been most evident in southern England, though not only in fruit-growing areas. Once established in cultivated land, the species might have been expected to become a major pest in orchards for, although primarily a seed-eater, even in its natural habitat it takes a greater proportion and variety of buds, and for a longer period each year, than does any other European bird. Indeed it is well adapted to do so in bill structure, feeding technique and digestive system, having a shorter, broader beak and a relatively longer gut than other finches. All cultivated fruit trees, moreover, have buds of the size most acceptable to Bullfinches and are derived from tree-species whose buds are preferred under natural conditions.

Damage Reduction

Crop damage by any pest can be reduced either by protecting the crop itself (with some sort of enclosure, scaring device or repellent chemical), or by reducing the numbers of the pest. The latter can be achieved either by killing large numbers each year (by poisoning, shooting or trapping), or 'biologically' by adjusting the environment in some way so that the pest's population is held at a permanently reduced level.

Enclosing a fruit crop against Bullfinches is feasible in small gardens, but impracticable in large orchards; scaring devices (such as bangers) are effective only until the birds get used to them—which often takes only a few days; and all chemical deterrents applied so far to buds have achieved little or no lasting success, in part because Bullfinches eat only the small centres from buds and peel off the outer layers bearing the chemicals. Most chemicals are also washed off by rain, and when most needed (during cold weather) are difficult to handle as watery solutions: a systemic deterrent, that could be sprayed on to the ground and then taken up by the tree into its buds, might be more effective, but as yet has not been tried.

For reducing the numbers of Bullfinches directly, poisoning is undesirable because it is unselective and harmful to other wildlife, while shooting is expensive and time-consuming and incidentally damages the trees. Systematic nest destruction is in my experience so time-consuming as to be impracticable, and any way natural predators are far more effective. However, a group from the Ministry of Agriculture, Fisheries and Food have developed a trap that is not only effective, but also cheap, easy to operate and harmless to other animals. It consists of a baited wire box which catches the birds alive, so that they can later be disposed of humanely. Used with a decoy, this trap has so far proved much the best way of reducing damage.

Pest Control

In any such problem it is also desirable to learn what controls the numbers of the pest under natural conditions and to discover what factors influence the amount of damage. For these reasons I studied for six years the Bullfinches living in an area of mixed deciduous woodland, farmland and orchards near Oxford. Here the diet consisted mainly of buds for up to one third of each year, but at other times a great variety of seeds. In the woodland, at least four-fifths of the tree species and half the herbaceous plants provided food at one time or another. But these plants were not fed from in proportion to their abundance and some of the least common plants yielded the substantial part of the food. From May onwards, the most important seeds in the diet were dog's mercury, wych elm, birch, bramble, nettle, docks and ash. On nearby cultivated land, the birds ate mainly the seeds of various weeds, such as chickweed, dandelion, buttercups, sorrel, sow-thistle and fat-hen. In both habitats they fed their young on a mixture of seeds and small invertebrates, including caterpillars, spiders and small snails, the latter being de-shelled in the bill like seeds.

The winter seed diet was obtained almost entirely from two types of herbaceous plants, two shrubs and two trees. The crops of all these plants were produced in late summer and not replenished by further seed production during the winter. The seed crops of dock, nettle and bramble were fairly consistent in quantity from year to year, but those of privet, birch and ash varied greatly. This was especially true of ash, which in some years produced a tremendous profusion of seeds and in others none at all. Previously no animals were known to eat ash seeds in quantity and to my palate they were distasteful. Bullfinches, moreover, were extremely selective, feeding consistently from a few trees and leaving most untouched. As seeds became scarce during winter, and their variety restricted, buds became increasingly important in the bird's diet, especially those of hawthorn, but also of crab apple, wych elm and other trees. But feeding trials on captive birds showed that, in winter, Bullfinches could not maintain their weight on buds alone, neither those of native nor of orchard trees, and needed some seeds in order to survive. Only after the end of February when buds were larger and days were longer, could the birds subsist entirely on buds. It thus seemed likely that wild Bullfinches ate large numbers of buds in winter only when seeds were scarce, and to test this view I measured the seasonal decline in seed stocks in the woods each winter, and at the same time checked the neighbouring fruit farms for damage. The seeds disappeared from the various food plants during winter mainly through the activities of Bullfinches, but also many fell to the ground and were lost, and some of the birch seeds were eaten by other birds. But the basic pattern was simple and straightforward. In three years when the ash crop failed, the seeds of all other food-plants had disappeared, or almost disappeared, by mid-winter, and Bullfinches relied heavily on buds. In these years, damage on fruit farms was severe. In three other years when the ash crop was good, seeds lasted throughout the winter, and Bullfinches ate few buds before March. In these years damage on fruit farms was slight.

Ash Crop

From the fruit-grower's viewpoint, the seeds of ash are thus the most important winter food of Bullfinches as they are often the only alternative to buds at a time when other seeds have been eaten. Past records show that, in southern England, good ash crops usually occur every second year, with little or no seed produced in the intervening years. Replies to question-naires sent to fruit-growers in various areas showed that, as expected, most had suffered severe bud damage in their orchards only in the alternate years in which the ash crop failed. Also since the crop fluctuated in phase over the whole area, so did the amount of bud damage, and all areas suffered together.

It might be thought that one solution to the problem would

be to break in some way the biennual cropping of the ash so that seeds were available every year, or else to supply an alternative supply of seeds in the lean years. However, even if this were feasible, it would not be a satisfactory solution, for Bullfinches are almost certainly held in check by food shortage in the winters when seeds are scarce. As mentioned earlier, they cannot maintain themselves in mid-winter on buds alone, and around Oxford mortality was heaviest in those years without an ash crop for then most seeds had disappeared by January; that is, before buds were large enough to provide adequate nourishment. Hence, if food were provided artificially in the winters lacking ash seeds, Bullfinches might survive these winters in larger numbers than at present and increase to an even higher level set by this new food supply. Also, putting extra food in orchards might make the birds concentrate there in even greater numbers than at present.

Effective Control

The correlation between ash crops and bud damage does at least mean that fruit-growers can predict the years in which severe attacks are likely, and plan their control accordingly. When traps were first introduced, most growers concentrated their trapping in spring, when attacks were occurring and, although damage was reduced in this way, it was still severe. But from a better knowledge of the bird's ecology a more effective trapping programme was worked out. Seed stocks, remember, are not replenished during the winter. Hence the more numerous the birds in autumn the sooner they might be expected to consume these seeds and turn to buds, and the greater should be the damage. But by removing some birds in the autumn, natural seed stocks might be conserved, the date at which the birds turn to buds delayed, and the total damage reduced. So the plan was to trap in the autumn, in nearby woods and hedges, instead of spring in the orchards themselves. After successful preliminary trials on several farms in 1963, autumn trapping soon came into general use, and has resulted, in the years following, in much reduced damage. The method works because most Bullfinches move over only short distances (up to five miles), so immigration is limited, and because several of their important natural foods are not eaten regularly by other animals, so that if Bullfinches are removed, these foods last longer.

The method also has the minimum long-term effect on Bullfinch numbers, and thus largely satisfies the conservationist as well as the fruit grower. The totals caught by individual growers have not declined over the years so, although trapping has lessened damage, it has not apparently caused any long-term reduction in Bullfinch numbers. Its principal effect is to bring the main period of mortality forward from mid-winter (natural starvation) to early autumn (artificial control). But compared with individuals that die naturally, those killed by fruit growers contain a much higher proportion of first-year birds. For instance, from October to December 1964, the ratio of first year to older birds netted in woodland was 2:1 (which fits with the reproductive rate), whereas among nearly three hundred killed in orchards in the same months, first year birds outnumbered adults by 38 to 1. This is partly because young birds are easier to trap and partly because they move around more than older birds (as proved by ringing), so that more come within range. On an average fruit farm, a few hundred Bullfinches might be destroyed annually, but on a large farm in well wooded country over a thousand. This seems a lot, but even with birds moving over only five miles, the potential of a single trap extends over thirty-one square miles. Elsewhere in Europe Bullfinches are more migratory, but the suspicions of fruit-growers on the east coast of England that some come to winter in Britain alongside the resident population is not supported by ringing recoveries.

Biological Control

In the past, attempts to deal with pest species have often begun with the use (or misuse) of chemical deterrents and poisons. Most of these methods achieved little or no lasting success, but resulted in a wastage of public and private funds, pollution of soil or water, and an unnecessary destruction of other wildlife. Recent studies of several pest species have shown that any attempt at control is best preceded by a thorough knowledge of the pest's biology. But many consider such work a needless delay or of mere academic interest.

Swans

M. A. Ogilvie

Three species of swan inhabit Europe of which one, the Mute Swan, breeds widely in the western and central parts of the Continent while the other two, the Whooper Swan and Bewick's Swan, breed in the far north coming to more temperate areas for the winter.

The Mute Swan is resident in parts of its range, including the British Isles, northern France, Belgium, the Netherlands and Denmark, while farther east in Germany, southern Sweden, Poland and the Baltic States the birds are present only in the breeding season moving west and south-west for the winter. Apart from these countries small numbers are found in Switzerland, Austria, Greece, where they have been recently introduced, and around the Black Sea.

As well as being the most widespread of the three species, the Mute Swan is also the most numerous with a European population estimated at about 150,000. Of these roughly two-thirds live in the countries bordering the Baltic. Here vast winter gatherings occur particularly around the coasts of southern Sweden and eastern Denmark. As the winter becomes more severe the swans move west seeking open water, until by January they may virtually all be concentrated in Danish waters. In exceptionally cold weather, as in 1963, they will move further west still, into the Netherlands, and small numbers may even reach south-east England.

Mute on the Increase

This Baltic population of Mute Swans has increased enormously in the last fifty years. For example in the 1920s there were probably only five pairs breeding in Denmark where they had suffered from a long period of persecution. After being granted full protection in 1925 they began to recover their numbers and have not yet stopped growing. By 1954 there were nearly 800 pairs and at the latest count, in 1970, there were over 3,000. A most interesting result of this vast increase has been the abandonment of the traditional territorial breeding and the forming of colonies where up to 100 pairs breed with nests only a few yards apart. This has occurred along the coast where there is an abundance of food, aquatic vegetation, but a shortage of typical nesting territories of lengths of river and stream. Similar large increases in numbers have been reported from Germany, Poland and Sweden, while the species has colonised Latvia, Lithuania and Estonia in the last twenty years and from being something of a rarity in these countries is now breeding freely in many areas.

In Britain too we have seen Mute Swans increasing, though the trend has stopped in the last decade. In the mid-1950s the rate of increase was at its height and a census taken in 1955 and 1956 showed there were about 20,000 birds in England, Scotland and Wales. This growth continued until about 1959 before levelling out. Then in the hard winters of 1961–2 and 1962–3 the Mute Swans took quite a hard knock, their numbers being cut by up to a quarter. The birds have not really recovered from this drop and it has been suggested that their vulnerability to collisions with overhead powerlines is a sufficiently major cause of mortality to be holding the population at its present level. Certainly of every ringed bird that is recovered about half or even more are reported to have been found dead under overhead wires.

The Whooper Swan is also most numerous in the Baltic Sea in winter though its numbers do not match those of the Mute. In recent winters up to 12,000 have been counted in the shallow seas between Denmark and southern Sweden. These birds come from breeding grounds in northern Scandinavia and from the east across northern Russia. They do not penetrate far into the Arctic but are more or less confined to the wooded 'taiga' zone which extends south of the tundra. It is not known how far east the breeding range of European wintering Whoopers stretches but at some point in Siberia there is an invisible line to the west of which the swans migrate south-west to Europe and to the east of which they fly southeast to winter in Japan and China.

The Whooper Swans which winter in northern Britain and Ireland come not from the east but from Iceland to the northwest. Here there are an estimated 5,000 birds of which up to 4,000 winter in Britain. The remainder stay behind in Iceland finding open water on the great coastal lagoons in the south-east of the country or on those lakes into which thermal springs flow thus keeping them partially free of ice. If the winter in Iceland gets really bad the birds can always come to Britain even though it may be in January rather than the more common migration time of October.

Within Britain there is a considerable amount of movement with birds arriving on the northern coasts and then gradually moving further south and west. Some go direct to Ireland and others follow them if it gets very cold in Scotland. The Icelandic Whoopers do not seem to winter much further south than Yorkshire and it is probable, though yet to be proved, that Whoopers seen in southern England belong to the Scandinavian–Russian population. However ringing recoveries are still needed to confirm or deny this theory.

Out of Siberia

The rarest of the three swans is the Bewick's. The total population wintering in Europe is probably no more than five or six thousand. Their main breeding grounds lie far to the north-east in Siberia. Although small numbers are reported to breed almost throughout arctic Russia eastwards from the Finnish border, the principal concentrations are believed to be around the Kara Sea and on the Yamal Peninsula. Thus most of the swans have a journey of at least 2,500 miles each spring and autumn.

The winter headquarters of the Bewick's Swan has long been in the Netherlands but numbers in the British Isles have been increasing in the last few years and the latter may soon become the main wintering area. Counts over several years have shown the Bewick's Swan to be prepared to exploit new wintering areas and desert old ones rather more quickly than most waterfowl which are usually more traditional in their preferences. Sometimes the change has come because of pressure on an existing haunt which forces the birds to move, but an ability to explore and locate potential new areas also seems to exist. In this way Bewick's Swans first started wintering on the Ouse Washes in Cambridgeshire and Norfolk in the early 1950s. In recent years additional protection at this site has helped it become one of the foremost waterfowl wintering areas in Europe and the 1,200 Bewick's Swans that have been counted there at one time form Europe's largest flock.

Elsewhere in Britain the most extraordinary change in wintering habits of the Bewick's Swan has been on the Severn at Slimbridge. Here at the headquarters of the Wildfowl Trust over 400 swans crowd on to a small pool of a few acres, being fed corn thrice daily by a man with a barrow. Artificial feeding of the swans is also carried out on the Ouse Washes, but the birds were already present in large numbers whereas at Slimbridge the feeding has been a main cause behind the build up of a considerable flock. In the early 1960s up to twenty Bewick's were quite frequently seen at Slimbridge and were often attracted down into the Wildfowl Trust's enclosures by the presence of the tame birds there. Then in 1964 one area was closed to the public and protected from disturbance by screen walls. The swans soon became quite confiding and showed their trust by returning year after year, bringing their families and friends with them. From small beginnings of twenty-four birds in 1964, numbers rose rapidly with over 200 present at a time in 1967 and over 400 in 1970, at which level it has remained.

'Fingerprint' Face Patterns

It was Sir Peter Scott, sitting in his studio at Slimbridge with the wild Bewick's floating on the pool just outside the window, who realised that he could recognise individuals among the flock by their bill markings of black and yellow. The distribution of the two colours varied slightly, but distinctly, in each bird he could see. These 'face' markings were quickly conveyed to paper and so began a most fascinating study of individually recognisable swans that has now lasted more than ten years. Several hundred swans have been caught and ringed and this has proved, if proof were needed, that these face markings are like finger prints: each swan has a different pattern and there is no change in it as the bird grows older. Over the years known birds have returned to the pool with their mate and their cygnets of the year, introducing a new generation to the strange surroundings with buildings close in on two sides, but with the compensating regular supply of food. And gradually the watchers have seen the young ones grow up and start bringing families of their own.

The ability to recognise individuals out of a concourse of

seemingly completely identical birds adds a new dimension to any study of a species. Suddenly intimate details of family life and behaviour are revealed in a manner not apparent before. Thus the faithfulness of some birds has been shown, returning year after year arriving early each season in October and not departing until March. Such birds are obviously perfectly content to spend their winters at Slimbridge but there are many others which use it merely as a staging post on their way to or from other haunts. They may spend a day or two or even a week at Slimbridge but sooner or later they leave for somewhere else. Sometimes the alternative haunt may be quite close to Slimbridge, while other birds may be making for Ireland. Ringing has helped reveal the movements of some of the birds while they are away from Slimbridge because in order to identify them from bill patterns one needs to be rather closer than is possible in most places. Ringing has been done with large numbered plastic rings which can be read with a telescope at distances of up to 200 yards. Additionally some birds were marked with yellow dye on their tail feathers and these provided exciting reports from the Netherlands, Germany, Sweden and even Estonia as they winged their way eastwards on spring migration.

Speedy Fledging

The breeding habits of the three species of swan are fairly similar. All build large mound nests of vegetation. They do not carry the material to the nest but gather what is within reach piling it up all round to form a deep cup into which the eggs are laid. While Mute Swans will generally lay clutches of from five to ten eggs, Bewick's and Whoopers rarely lay more than five or six, often only four. The incubation period of the Mute Swan is about five weeks, and about four to four and a half weeks for the other two. Fledging in the Whooper and Bewick's is much quicker than in the Mute as the young of the two former species have to be able to migrate away from the breeding grounds before the autumn freeze comes. In the case of the Bewick's it only takes six weeks for the young to be on the wing, and about eight to nine for the Whooper, whereas young Mute Swans may not be flying until they are about twenty weeks old.

Both parent swans assiduously look after their young. Only the female incubates though the male occasionally sits on the nest when she is off feeding, or before the clutch is complete. Whilst incubation is in progress the male acts as a guard standing or swimming around never far from the nest and ready to defend it against predators or even human intruders. The male Mute Swan with his wings raised and neck feathers all puffed up is an awesome sight which has successfully driven off many a trespasser. The two others do not have the ability to inflate themselves in quite the same aggressive posture but they will open their wings wide and stretch upright to look as large as possible. The Whooper Swan will actually adopt this stance if a light aircraft flies low over its nest.

Once the young have hatched both parents look after them, pulling up vegetation from under the water or down from banks. The young are vegetarian almost from the start though they may take small water insects as well. In the case of the migratory swans, the family stays together as a unit right through the first winter and the young leave the wintering area and embark upon the spring migration with their parents. However, before they reach the breeding grounds the young stop off at some suitable haunt while the parents fly on alone. In some cases they all return to the breeding site where the parent birds chase the young away. In the Mute Swan, those parents which remain on their breeding territory throughout the winter generally drive their young away as soon as the latter lose their brown juvenile plumage and get their white first year feathering. Those adults which winter away from the territory leave with their cygnets but the family unit breaks up before the parents leave in the spring, and the young remain in the wintering haunt usually in a flock with immatures from other families.

Non-breeding Flocks

The young ones are not capable of breeding until they are three or even four years old and until this age is reached they flock with other immature non-breeding birds spending their summer in some area away from the breeding grounds. This is always some safe place with ample supplies of food because for three to four weeks each summer the birds become flightless during their annual moult. All the main wing feathers are shed at once and until they grow again the swans are confined to the one area. The breeding birds moult when they have young, the male first and then when he is about ready to fly again the female moults, so that there is always one fully winged adult to defend the brood. During the winter the immatures flock in the same places as the adults and the Slimbridge study has revealed that second winter Bewick's Swans often meet up with their parents again and stay through the winter with them even though there is a new brood of cygnets present as well. Third and even fourth year birds have been recorded doing this.

Pairing takes place when the young birds are in their second year and young Mute Swan pairs may adopt a territory for the summer, though without making a nest or laying any eggs. Then they will return the following year to breed. Once mated, swans are proverbially faithful to each other though

Page 125   (*above*) House Martins making mud pellets with which to build their nests—the bird on the right is about to fly off with a completed pellet; (*below*) the lofty grey boughs of the beeches on the Hanger

Page 126 (*above*) The illegal and barbarous pole trap; (*right*) dead Tawny Owl, victim of a pole trap

intensive studies of ringed Mute Swans in Britain have shown that there are occasional cases of divorce when a swan will take a new mate even though his original mate is still alive. However, this is reassuringly rare.

Another important aspect of swan life, particularly of the northern breeding species, is their breeding performance. Most arctic nesting birds are very variable in the number of young that they manage to raise from year to year and Bewick's and Whooper Swans are no exception. Mute Swans which breed in more temperate areas are not subject to this in anything like the same way. The Arctic has many advantages as a breeding place for swans, not least its vastness and consequent freedom from disturbance. There is also ample food and water and though the summer is very short the birds have managed to shorten their breeding cycle sufficiently to squeeze it into the brief period between the spring thaw in late May and the autumn freeze-up in September. However, this means that over a very wide area all the swans have to start breeding at pretty well the same time. Then if there is a sudden spell of bad weather, as can so easily happen in the Arctic, and it coincides with egg-laying or hatching, there will be a very widespread and considerable loss of eggs or young. Thus in a bad year hardly any swans will rear young while in a good one the majority of pairs will do so. This breeding performance is usually measured by counting the number of young birds in a flock and expressing it as a percentage of the whole. The average brood size is also noted, which is quite easy to do as the birds stay in family parties within a flock and the two parents and their cygnets move as a cohesive unit among the other swans. The range of percentages of young is from under 5 per cent in a very poor year to over 45 per cent in a very good one. Similarly the average size of broods will vary from just over one to four or more.

Threats in Winter

Such great variations in breeding success will naturally have their effect on the total number of birds making up the population. A run of bad years will cause a decrease while one or two good ones can result in a great upsurge. Clearly the swans have long since adapted to the rigours of the weather on their arctic breeding grounds and over a long period there should be no major rise or fall in numbers. There are, however, other influences at work, in particular, adverse ones on the wintering grounds where wetland habitat is under constant threat. All the swans like to graze on wet pastureland in winter, and although winter flooding is recognised as being beneficial to the growth of grass, it is considered much more economic to prevent the flooding altogether and thus be able to convert at least some of the land to arable. This has occurred in countless river valleys and low-lying areas throughout Europe, with drainage authorities and engineers appearing to regard any flooding in their area as an affront to their professional competence.

Unfortunately in arguments involving the production of better farmland against the loss of wetland habitat for swans and other waterfowl, the birds almost always lose. Only in the last few years have conservation bodies become strong and rich enough to be able to save some of these areas by purchase or lease. They may not, however, be able to save enough and it is necessary for the land to be managed to make it more productive of vegetation for the birds and to be backed up by artificial feeding as required.

The beauty of Mute Swans and the wildness of Whoopers and Bewick's appeal to many people, not just bird-watchers. Their present status and future prospects seem fairly assured but constant vigilance and effort will be needed to safeguard them in the years to come. Who can deny that they are worth it?

Selborne 1774-1974

Ian Beames

Gilbert White and Selborne—White was the father of British ornithology and Selborne was, and still is, his village. Even now the words of Gilbert White are written right across the landscape. In his very first letter he says '. . . a vast hill of chalk, rising three hundred feet above the village, and is divided into a sheep down, a high wood and a long hanging wood called the Hangar. The covert of this eminence is altogether beech, the most lovely of all forest trees.' The graceful beeches soar into the sky above Selborne still.

White was born in Selborne on 18 July 1720 and came to live at 'The Wakes' in the main street of the village when he was about seven years old. It was his home until his death at the age of seventy-three in June 1793. He went to school in Basingstoke and from thence he went to Oriel College, Oxford, where he obtained his Fellowship in 1744 and his Master's Degree two years later. He held a variety of curacies in local parishes but his beloved Selborne belonged to Magdalen College and he was never able to be its vicar—although he was four times curate.

The Wakes (see plate, p 108) is now a museum and as one stands in White's study looking out across the wide lawns, one sheds two hundred years. The Blackbird sitting on her four eggs in the climbing rose just outside the window, the Swallow skimming low across the dewy lawn, and the Chaffinch singing from the great yew tree must be just what White would have seen on a fine June morning. A Spotted Flycatcher uses a fence post as a perch to flit out and catch passing insects. This year there is a pair breeding in the ramblers on a nearby wall. Two hundred years ago White said 'the flycatcher has not yet appeared—it usually breeds in my vine.'

Downland Village

Selborne is still a quiet little Hampshire village—a typical downland village with its buildings set along one main street. Admittedly several of them now sell afternoon teas, others antiques and yet more are labelled galleries, but the House Martins which nest under many of the eaves must have been doing so for hundreds of years. Approaching Selborne from the east one comes to White's 'rocky hollow lane'—a deep cutting through the freestone, at its deepest near the village with great chunks of rock jutting out somewhat menacingly at the road. The remaining banks are covered with a dense vegetation including a wide variety of ferns which White specially mentions. Today there are male fern, bracken, black spleen wort, hartstongue, buckler fern, common spleenwort and polypody—seven species in all.

Selborne stands at the junction of several different types of soil—in particular the Upper Greensand to the north-east and the chalk to the south-west, and each has different plants and animal life. The most obvious land mass is the great hill of chalk which rises high above the village to the south. This is the famous Beech Hanger and is part of the chalk scarp which stretches for fifty miles across Wiltshire and Dorset and as far again into Surrey and Kent.

Hibernation

If you climb the Hanger from the west you pass several old thatched cottages teeming with House Martins. We know now that the Martins migrate late in the autumn to Africa—ringing recoveries and observation have showed how and by what routes they travel—but White thought it possible that they hibernated, although his careful observations gave him some cause for doubt. Many of his contemporaries, however, were totally against migration and very much for the 'hibernation' theory.

White was fascinated by migrating birds—as indeed are many thousands of modern ornithologists. Many of his writings are concerned with the subject. He was particularly attached to his Ring Ouzels which appeared every year on the Downs in early spring and again around Michaelmas in autumn. They were so regular in their appearances that he wrote '. . . these birds—from the observations of three springs and two autumns are most punctual in their return and exhibit a new migration un-noticed by the writers.'

White, by carefully noting down every observation (a text book lesson for every modern ornithologist) was able to show that many birds did migrate. About the Blackcap he says '. . . Mr. Stillingfleet makes a question whether the Blackcap be a bird of passage or not: I think there is no doubt of it for, in April, in the first fine weather they come trooping all at once into these parts but are never seen in the winter.'

By 1773 White was convinced of the phenomenon of migration and said so quite clearly in a letter to Daines Barrington. 'You are, I know, no great friend of migration,' he wrote. 'But we must not, I think, deny migration in general; because migration certainly does subsist in some places, as my brother in Andalusia has fully informed me. During spring and fall, myriads of the Swallow kind traverse the straits (Gibraltar) from North to South and South to North according to the season—and these vast migrations consist not only of hirundines but Bee-Eaters, Hoopoes, thrushes and many of our soft-billed summer birds of passage.'

Ringing Recovery

In this selfsame letter White gives us one of the first ringing recoveries recorded: '. . . as some people were shooting in the parish of Trotten in Sussex they killed a duck in that dreadful winter of 1708–9 with a silver collar about its neck, on which were engraven the arms of the King of Denmark.'

In 1973 the thatch of the cottages looks a little incongruous lined with colour television aerials, and the harsh clatter of a bulldozer clearing a building plot soon destroys thoughts of two hundred years before. Up the path at the foot of the western end of the Hanger there are large clumps of Jack-by-the-hedge among the vegetation. Careful examination reveals the minute bright eggs of the Orange-tip butterfly—one egg per plant because the caterpillars are carnivorous. Here too there is a constantly changing flock of House Martins at a little muddy pool in the track, collecting building supplies for the nests under the thatched eaves of the village (see plate, p 125).

About a quarter of a mile from the end of the village the path begins to mount rapidly into the beech Hanger itself—the undergrowth thins out and the lofty grey boughs lift gracefully into the air overhead (see plate, p 125). The sunlight percolates through intermittently and there are larger expanses of open ground covered in dead leaves. Here and there among leaf litter are bird's nest orchids, uncommon saprophytic plants growing on the decaying leaf mould and containing no chlorophyll. A lot of bedstraw grows mainly along the paths.

The birds of these woods are not so numerous in summer as those of the oak forests nearby. They are either hole nesting species, beech provides some excellent if sparse hole nest sites, or small birds of the leaf canopy which breed in the clearings or on the wood edge.

Common Bird Census

A bird census through the Hanger on 2 June 1973 produced the following records of singing males:

Chaffinch	8	Robin	2
Wren	7	Wood Warbler	2
Blue Tit	7	Willow Warbler	2
Blackbird	7	Mistle Thrush	2
Chiffchaff	5	Jackdaw	1
Woodpigeon	4	Starling	1
Blackcap	3	Whitethroat	1
Great Tit	2		

Gilbert White was the original discoverer of 'the three species of willow-wren'—and still they sing to the tourists from the Selborne woods. The Chiffchaff with its monotonous note—White noted 'it arrives in March and chirps to September.' White's Middle Willow Wren—the Willow Warbler, he noted as 'arrives the middle of April—a sweet plaintive note'. Of the Largest Willow Wren, the Wood Warbler of which he was discoverer, he says 'It is a size larger than the other two and the yellow green of the upper part of the body is more vivid and the belly a clearer white. It haunts only the tops of trees in the high beechen woods and makes a sibilous, shimmering noise.'

Along the tracks of these woods are roe deer slots—prints in the mud—fresh from the dawn. They are quite numerous around here now but in White's day they did not exist. Pennant

133

himself, to whom White wrote half of his 'Letters' states in his *British Zoology* (1776) 'the species no longer exists in any part of Great Britain except in the Scottish Highlands.' Probably the easiest place to see roe is at Selborne along the edge of Dorton Stream to the north-east. After about half a mile Dorton Lane opens out into large groves of beech. Dawn and dusk are the best times. Gilbert White would soon have seen them. The roe deer was re-established during the nineteenth century and has spread quickly over much of southern and central England.

Great Bustards

In comparing Selborne 1774 with Selborne 1974 it is important to remember that where there were only cart tracks great arterial roads now run, where small roads are now found there were only paths. Thus the main difference is that the countryside—then a whole unit—is now divided by concrete into many smaller ecological units, each capable of supporting less. In the first few letters written by White to describe the area it is learned that 'Selborne Manor abounds with Partridges, Pheasants, Hares, Quails and Landrails.' Partridges are certainly rare now, hares are few, Quails are only a trickle of passing visitors and Landrails or Corncrakes have virtually retreated to the northern islands. Ravens bred in the forest—there are none there now. There were Choughs 'all along the cliffs of Sussex' and Great Bustards. Kites and Buzzards bred regularly on the South Downs. Wheatears and Whinchats were very numerous breeding birds and Stone Curlews were in abundance on all of the local downland. Spain and Portugal are the most likely places for Bustards now and the Chough now lives no nearer than the cliff-bound coast of South Wales, and even there it is a rare bird.

The Pheasant fortunately is still much in evidence. They are, after all, easier to shoot than Partridges so their survival is assured. Surprisingly there are still one or two Buzzards inhabiting the woods—remnants of an attempt to re-establish them when nine were released at Witley Park in Surrey in 1939.

Wheatears and Whinchats are passage migrants to the uplands and breed only infrequently. The Stone Curlew still breeds on the Hampshire Downs but its population is sparse—while the Kite, like the Chough, is only found in the fastnesses of the Welsh hills.

Not everything is for the worse, however. Through the green woodlands of Selborne comes the harsh 'tchack' of the Great Spotted Woodpecker, a much more numerous bird now than it was, and the Goldcrest—White's 'Golden-crowned Wren, whose crown glitters like burnished gold—as rare a bird as any that we have'—is frequently seen along the woodland paths and appears to breed in the conifers of St Mary's Churchyard.

Martins over the Zig-Zag

One needs to pay several visits to Selborne to appreciate the subtleties and pleasures of White's rural life. These are the days of high speed car trips to see the Western Sandpiper at Rainham or the Courser at Cley—very satisfying rarity hunting! But stand in White's study at his window and look long over the quiet lawn to the swaying beeches of the Hanger, or sit by the little brook which chatters over the stones and swirls under the banks to the east of the village and wait while the Water Vole peers cautiously out to look at you. This is the very stuff of Gilbert White who sat at this stream and watched the Voles, probably at the selfsame place.

At the very top of the Hanger the views back into the village

135

several hundreds of feet below are superb. White's study window is probably the most prominent feature—closely followed by the radar dish aerials of the Royal Air Force station two miles to the north. House Martins and Swifts hawk along the steep wooded slopes in squadrons, picking off the insects rising on the warm air currents wafting up and over the scarp from the meadows below. As they reach the south-eastern end of the Hanger above White's celebrated Zig-Zag path they peel off in echelons and zoom down into the valley to hurtle low over the village.

In the beech woods on the flat summit of the Hanger a tiny weasel dashed across the wide path, its lithe body nearly flat on the ground. Like all weasels, having gained cover it stopped, curious to see what had disturbed it. Characteristically it stood on its hind legs and peered over the intervening grass. By its size, only about eight inches long, it was a female—out hunting for its kittens perhaps. Now we know that the male weasel is much bigger than the female; two or three inches in fact, and often nearly twice as heavy. In White's time many people thought that there were two distinct species because of their difference in size. White himself doubted it saying 'this piece of intelligence can be little depended upon but further enquiry will be made.' Next in size above the weasel is the stoat with its black-tipped tail and next again is the polecat, now a rare carnivore restricted to Wales but relatively numerous in Hampshire in 1773.

Harvest Mouse Described

White's powers of accurate observation are well shown in his studies of the harvest mouse. He was not only an ornithologist but a skilled general naturalist—curious about everything. He was the first person to describe the harvest mouse, still found in Selborne in the hedges and meadows especially along the Dorton Stream, although they are rare. Their habits have changed somewhat in two hundred years. They are found less often in wheat fields—probably because of the advent of mechanical harvesting. They are creatures of the stalk zone, that part of the thickest herbage usually a foot or two off the ground in ditches and reed beds. The marshy meadows and hedgerows near the stream are ideal sites and an hour's searching produced two old nests. White described their habits perfectly 'they are much smaller than the *Mus domesticus* (house mouse) of Ray and have more of the squirrel colour— they never enter houses, abound in harvest and build their nests amidst the straws of corn or in thistles. One of these nests I procured this autumn—composed of blades of wheat, round and the size of a cricket ball, suspended in the head of a thistle.'

White's mammology did not stop there—his observations included most of the common species, including the hedgehog which abounded in his garden. Judging by the number of corpses on the roads around the district they still do though the hazards are more numerous now.

Note that White says the harvest mouse is 'more of the squirrel colour'—red squirrels in 1773 of course since the grey squirrel was not introduced from America until a hundred years later. There are no red squirrels at Selborne now. The nearest ones are isolated colonies on the Isle of Wight and Brownsea Island in Poole Harbour in Dorset. The grey squirrel, much more hardy and adaptable than its European cousin, is common enough round Selborne where it seems to like the old oaks to the east of the churchyard particularly.

White was also the first person to describe the noctule bat. He says, in a letter to Pennant 'The Great Large Bat ranges very high for its food—now this is exactly the case with the Swifts. From hence I would conclude that these hirundines and the large bats are supported by some sorts of high flying gnats or scarabs.' In 1771 White at last procured a 'Great Large Bat' which he named *vespertilio altivolans*, because it flew high in the air, commenting that on fine summer evenings they could be seen flying with the swifts, hunting insects.

Beech woods are now well-known haunts of noctule bats which live in small colonies, usually of ten to twenty animals, in holes in trees. There are clearly one or two such colonies in Selborne Hanger itself because they may still be seen darting at speed after beetles high above the trees in the early dusk on most fine summer days, while Swifts scream across the sky.

Walking on through the high beech arches towards Selborne Common one realises that the bird song has increased in volume, mainly because there is more undergrowth. The beeches thin out and there are oaks, ash and many hawthorns and other bushes. Nightingales, Blackcaps, Willow Warblers and Whitethroats all sing in profusion on the edge of the Common. White called the Blackcap 'a delicate songster' while of the Whitethroat he wrote 'the note of the Whitethroat—is harsh and displeasing and in July and August they bring their broods into the gardens and make great havoc among the summer fruit.'

A Great Yew

There is a Nature Trail which starts at the little village green called the Plestor, immediately across the main street from the Wakes, where a leaflet describing the Trail can be obtained. Leaving the green one immediately enters the churchyard of St Mary's and is confronted by an enormous yew tree which now has a girth of over twenty-five feet, nearly two and a half feet more than when White measured it. It must have stood here when King Harold was slain at Hastings. There are other large trees here, mainly conifers, including an atlas cedar, noble fir and several cypresses and spruces. They are a favourite haunt of tits, especially Coal Tits, and Goldcrests. All of these trees are 'quick growers' and were planted after White's time.

The footpath through the churchyard leads to a gate and passes into a long meadow called Church Litten, which slopes down to Dorton Stream. There is a rookery in the trees on the far side of the valley. By mid-summer the young Rooks are fledged and away in the fields. At the foot of the slope is Dorton Cottage, a lovely old house which stood in White's time. It is half surrounded by woods and a stream runs through the garden. There are two enormous oak trees standing in the meadow just before the cottage. One is a common oak while the other is a sessile oak. A large growth of polypody fern can be seen in the left hand one. In early summer these two trees support a breeding population of two pairs of Jackdaws, two pairs of Starlings, and a pair each of Great Tits, Blue Tits and Nuthatches.

A few yards further on the stream chatters along by the side of a wood and under a little footbridge. Grey Wagtails can be seen here. White saw an otter here too and was much surprised. Otters are even rarer now in the south of England.

Still No Minnows

Half an hour with a child's net and a jam-jar in this stream is sufficient to produce several sticklebacks and the odd bull-head or two. Minnows seem to be non-existent. White makes this comment 'A person, by my order, has searched our brooks— he found the Stickleback in plenty—this morning in a basket I packed a little earthen pot and in it some Sticklebacks, some Lamperns and some Bull-heads—but I could procure no Minnows.' Evidently the stream has changed little.

Some two hundred yards farther on the path breaks out of the wood into a dry valley which slopes down towards the stream. Near the stream banks the ground becomes very marshy and there are lots of tall yellow iris and marsh thistles. Mole-hills are much in evidence along here. Several lines of them run through the woods and out into the grassy meadows.

The Nature Trail runs along the path through the woods parallel to the stream. It is sheltered here and a particularly good place for birds and insects. Chiffchaff, Willow Warbler, Blackcap, Whitethroat and Garden Warbler can all be heard singing and there are frequent parties of Bullfinches. In late summer Greenfinches come to feed on the teazel and thistle-heads.

The woods are mixed deciduous, full of old trees and with many sites for hole-nesting birds. Blue and Great Tits are numerous and Coal Tits are often seen. All three species of woodpecker are seen here; the Great Spotted Woodpecker by far the most numerous, the Green Woodpecker and the Lesser Spotted Woodpecker being infrequently encountered. Nuthatches and Tree Creepers are often seen, especially with the tit flocks from late summer onwards and it is probably hereabouts that White tried experiments with hazel nuts to see how the Nuthatch opened them. 'We have often placed nuts', he writes, 'in the chink of a gatepost where Nuthatches have been known to haunt and have always found that those birds have readily penetrated them.' White also noted that they make a rapping noise that can be heard at a considerable distance.

There are many flowers along this part of the path with woodruff, violets, stitchwort, thistles, vetches and speedwells. Consequently there are lots of insects, especially butterflies. There are scores of meadow browns, gatekeepers and wall browns in the sunny spots. Speckled woods prefer the dappled sunlight among the trees. Small tortoiseshells and peacocks lay their eggs on the clumps of stinging nettles, the peacocks preferring the isolated clumps in the meadows. If one is lucky there are occasional white admirals which glide gracefully along the wood edge looking for bramble blossom to feed from and for honeysuckle on which to lay their eggs.

Still the Same Flowers

At a distance of about half a mile from the churchyard the Nature Trail emerges into Combe Meadow, a wide field which slopes gently to the stream banks. The ground is wet and marshy and Snipe can be seen here in the spring—usually on migration. Giant horsetail grows in the boggy parts, along with rushes, sedges and meadow sweet. Crossing the meadow, with Skylarks singing high overhead, the farthest point of the Trail passes over the bridge at Dorton Stream. There are trout here and the water is deeper. The Trail crosses the bridge and river into a long damp beech woodland, the paths are muddy over 'clay-with-flints' soil, the remains of a washed-out chalk soil. Spotted orchids, birds nest orchids and green hellebore grow here. White noted all of these at this exact spot. This is an excellent place for roe deer, whose tracks can always be seen in the muddy path.

Back towards the village—this time on the opposite banks of the stream—watching for water voles along the banks and a variety of fungi in the leaf-litter. The path leads out of the wood past Dorton Cottage again and quite quickly back into the village opposite 'The Wakes'.

The parish of Selborne was very large and, as White says in his introductory letters, took in much of Wolmer Forest and Oakhanger—while to the north it abutted Alice Holt Forest, now the Forestry Commission Research Station. White was fascinated to learn that there were fallow deer and only fallow deer in Alice Holt; while there were red deer in Wolmer—and only red deer. There are still fallow deer in Alice Holt but the red deer have long since gone, and there are roe deer now in both Forests.

Oakhanger Ponds are still in existence—just! In 1795 they were recorded as covering 263 acres. Today they are totally silted up; the stream bed flowing into them is virtually dry. Almost all of the 200 acres is a dense tangle of sallows and willows. Where these thin out reed mace is still growing in quantity. Open water can be measured in a few square yards and the most frequently encountered birds are Willow Warblers and Blackcaps.

Wolmer Pond lies on the edge of Wolmer Forest. It was apparently much larger in White's time being then nearly a half a mile by a quarter. It is probably half that size now, but in summer there are occasional Sedge Warblers here, a bird first described by White in his letters 'It is a size less than the Grasshopper-lark, over each eye there is a milk white stroke.'

The Pond has a very meagre breeding population of birds with a few Mallard, Yellowhammers, Reed Buntings and Skylarks. The surrounding bog supports the passing Lapwing and Snipe but it is doubtful if it can now be said of Wolmer 'on the face of this vast expanse of waters—lie all day long in the winter season vast flocks of ducks, teals and wigeon.'

Chatter of Machine-guns

Wolmer Forest is much as White described it, with one important exception. The 'forest stone', chunks of iron-stone, still lie scattered over the 'hungry sandy barren waste'. It is still a vast tract of pine, gorse and heather—and bare sand. But the most noticeable thing about Wolmer is the chatter of machine-gun and small arms fire, and the occasional crump of

Page 143 (*above*) Caged Brambling, Siskin and Yellowhammers;
(*below*) Avocets

a shell, for Wolmer Forest is now War Department property and is used as a firing range.

If Gilbert White were alive now he would probably still live in Selborne. It is still in the heart of the countryside, it is quiet and beautiful, and above all its wildlife and flowers are still there. The Wood Warbler still sings from the highest and most graceful beech woods, and the Ouzels still appear on the Downs at Michaelmas with regularity. There is just as much to absorb the life-time of a curious naturalist, although to study the Ouzels and the other migrations he would probably use the Oakhanger radar dish!

Traps, gins and other nasties

Richard Porter

When I joined the RSPB staff some five years ago to handle the investigation and enforcement of the Protection of Birds Act, I felt as though I was entering a dying profession. A certain naivety and lack of experience probably led me to believe so but, at the same time, most people seemed to feel that such things as wholesale bird trapping, egg-collecting, destruction of birds of prey and the use of pole traps were phases in the history of the RSPB and were now on the way out. Sad to say this is not true. Although one cannot directly compare today with what was happening at the turn of the century, I hope this article will show that there is much cause for concern, particularly when it is remembered that as the threats from pollution, pesticide poisoning, habitat destruction and such-like increase, so man's direct persecution of birds and their eggs is likely to have a more serious effect.

Eggs for Sale

Egg-collecting, for instance, was in its heyday in the latter part of the last century and in the early part of this one, and was then considered not only socially acceptable but the basis of much of the ornithological research being carried out. In many ways it was the forerunner of the sophisticated surveys and enquiries that conservation organisations carry out today.

Eggs also fetched quite high prices on the market and there were many oological catalogues advertising eggs for sale as well as a number of publications devoted solely to their collecting. Today all eggs of British breeding birds are protected by law except those of some sixteen species including Crows, Rooks, Magpies, Jackdaws, House Sparrows, Woodpigeons and Starlings whose activities at times are considered harmful.

Yet egg-collecting is still rife among a group of about 200 people ranging in social status from brigadiers and company directors to sheet metal workers.

Enquiries carried out in 1973 revealed that they tried all manner of means in their search for eggs, particularly of our rare and endangered breeding birds. During that year we found over 200 Little Tern eggs, all taken in the last few years, two clutches of Goshawks and Peregrines, fifteen clutches of Golden Eagles, five clutches of Kites, two clutches of Avocets, ten clutches of Dotterel, fifteen clutches of Slavonian Grebe and Red-throated Divers all during the course of raids on the houses of collectors whose activities we had been following. One person had no fewer than 26,000 eggs in cabinets throughout his house, though fortunately this was exceptional. The prosecutions which followed showed that magistrates were concerned about this plundering of the countryside. One person from Coventry was fined £155 plus £300 costs; a man from Hereford £75 plus £150 costs for taking Kites' eggs. All the way down, even to the smallest cases, we felt that the courts were on the side of the birds.

Strange as it might seem there is little evidence to suggest that there is a market for eggs today. Most collectors want to take their own eggs and 'participate' in the 'excitement' of the challenge which involves breaking the law. To swap or buy is cheating. I remember a case not so long ago of a gamekeeper in northern England who took a clutch of Merlin's eggs for a collector. When the collector arrived he took the eggs and walked the five or six miles back over difficult moorland to replace them in the nest so that he could take them for himself! Another person whom we prosecuted admitted that he had never been beaten by any bird's nest no matter how difficult the climb.

Spotless Collection

Another collector's item is the stuffed bird. I have on my desk a stuffed Black-necked Grebe, now a paper-weight, that had once swum happily on a London reservoir until it was identified as a £20 cheque by a passing taxidermist—there is an interesting saga attached to that incident. A few years ago on a Monday morning (always a bad time) I was 'phoned by a man who had tried to buy the Grebe. Evidently he had paid cash for the bird, but the taxidermist who had shot it did not hand it over. Obviously a case for the civil courts, but I had a witness to an offence against the Protection of Birds Act. After a few more telephone calls I had arranged with the police to take out a search-warrant and was off to visit the taxidermist in the company of a superintendent of police. I was warned that it might be rather tricky as the last time the police had to visit this particular person he had barricaded himself in the house and threatened them with a shotgun. Fortunately, on this day things were more reasonable and we managed to get all the evidence we required to take him to court.

But the most fascinating thing about the enquiry was seeing the inside of his house: it was an ideal set for a Steptoe film with the exception of a small room upstairs where he held his collection of trophies. Stepping over a half-stuffed fish carcass on the landing, I was stunned to see an array of beautifully mounted waders, warblers, thrushes, finches, flycatchers all peering out from their glass cabinets on which I could not see so much as a finger print. Unfortunately, despite my suspicions to the contrary, I was unable to prove that any had been recently taken. Under the Act is it not an offence just to have illegally taken birds—alive or dead—in one's possession. It is only an offence if they have been recently taken which, as you can imagine, is always hard to prove. I often stop and give silent thanks to our legislators in making our job so easy!

Taxidermists are on the increase and again we have been fairly successful in prosecutions against those who have been taking or receiving birds which have been illegally shot. The current popularity of stuffed birds in a home is no doubt linked to the boom in the antique trade and as long as there are people prepared to harbour a stuffed Bittern, Buzzard or Barn Owl in a glass cabinet in their studies there will always be people prepared to go out and shoot them.

The Fancy

The live bird, too, has a price-tag. Every week various magazines have advertisements offering British birds for sale. Now the law demands in the case of smaller birds—those that are prized by aviculturists and bird exhibitors—that the bird must be aviary bred and close-ringed before it is eligible for sale. Many of the advertised species are in fact aviary bred and close-ringed (ABCR) but a number are not, as prosecutions taken by ourselves or the RSPCA have shown. Indeed, it is true to say that of all the enquiries we make in the course of a year, more are in the field of small bird-trapping and selling than any other. Species that are most commonly trapped include Greenfinches, Goldfinches, Chaffinches, Siskins and Yellow-hammers (see plate, p 143), and one particular advertiser in the last three years has included Waxwings, Bramblings, Wheatears, Twites, Yellow Wagtails, Grey Wagtails, Song Thrushes and Pied Flycatchers among the numerous species he claims to have bred in such numbers as to allow the offspring to be sold.

Again, magistrates are now taking a realistic view of such offences. At Sutton Coldfield a trapper was fined £175 plus £74 costs in January of 1973, while in May a man from Cannock was fined £80 plus £11 costs for attempting to trap Siskins, Bullfinches and Redpolls. In Hull in July fines of £80 plus £23 costs were imposed on a bird fancier for trapping and being in possession of three Redpolls, four Greenfinches, a Goldfinch and a Brambling.

If small birds are the bread and butter of the market then birds of prey are the cream. They fetch high prices and there are always people prepared to illegally take them from a nest in Britain or import them from abroad. The latter is now illegal without a licence.

Barbaric Traps

The most barbaric practice which still exists in Britain must surely be that of pole trapping. Three years ago the RSPB started a campaign against the destruction of birds of prey and owls that were being regularly shot, poisoned or pole trapped in the interest of Pheasant, Partridge and Grouse shooting. We were told by the shooting fraternity that such activities were things of the past, yet in three years we have made, or assisted in, enquiries on nearly 200 estates in Britain where birds of prey and owls have been killed, and found no fewer than 180 pole traps! Quite appalling when you consider that this instrument was made illegal over seventy years ago.

What does one of these traps look like, how does it work? A circular steel or galvanised wire spring trap is placed on the top of a pole, some six or seven feet high and secured in position by a short chain. The post is sited in an area where it will act as a favourite resting place for hawks and owls so that they can spy out the land in search of small rodents. When a bird alights upon the trap, which fits neatly on top of the post, the jaws spring up and seize it by the legs. Being non-selective, if a Blackbird or Thrush happens to alight, it will be caught by the body and the life rapidly squeezed out of it. But the bird of prey or owl will hang upside down with smashed legs until slowly it dies (see plates, p 126).

These traps are foul objects, supposedly protecting game chicks from the exaggerated marauding of owls and other predators, but I am afraid I could not resist a smile when last year I was sent a photograph of a pheasant caught in a pole trap in Oxfordshire. I did not feel a full-scale enquiry was needed—that little incident would soon get them banned from the estate!

It would be nice to think that more landowners and shooting syndicates took as tough a line as Lord Barnard did in 1900 (at a time when virtually no protection laws existed) when he issued the following instructions:

MEMORANDUM OF
INSTRUCTIONS TO GAMEKEEPERS
Game-watchers, Woodmen and others
employed on Lord Barnard's Estates.

———

Rare birds or animals (including Peregrine Falcons, larger Seagulls, Badgers, etc) must never be destroyed without special instructions.

Owls of all kinds, Kestrels (or Windhovers), Buzzards and smaller Seagulls must not on any account be destroyed.

Where rats, mice, voles etc. are numerous, Weasels should be preserved.

———

Pole traps are forbidden.

Raby Castle   February, 1900.

151

Digging for birds

Cyril Walker

The majority of palaeontologists now agree that birds evolved from one of the great dinosaurian orders (namely the Saurischia) during the early part of the Jurassic period about 180 million years ago. Unfortunately, the fossil record is incomplete and one can only guess at how the avian form developed from the reptilian stock. Opinions differ however, as to what 'pre-avis' looked like. Some authorities say that this animal had an arboreal habit and began its attempts at flight by gliding from tree to tree, while others say that it was a ground-living, running and leaping animal, which increased the lengths of its leaps by use of elongated forelimbs. It is difficult to choose between the arguments and the truth is probably to be found between the two.

The fragile nature of bird bones (which are thin-walled and hollow) naturally reduces the chances of them being preserved as well as the other vertebrates and their fossil record suffers accordingly. Probably the best medium for preserving bird remains is mud which can encase the bones to form a matrix that may preserve the bone completely. As bird remains are more effectively preserved where they have settled into sea and lake beds, there is a bias towards those birds which live in an aquatic environment. Further, larger and stronger bones are more likely to withstand the rigours of fossilisation, and so it is also the larger animals which have a greater chance of being preserved.

Over 1,500 fossil birds have now been described. Most of these are from younger horizons between 10 million and 12,000 years ago, and are closely related to the avifauna of today, thus giving the palaeontologist only a poor idea of their lines of evolution. As would be expected, the further back one goes in geological time the rarer bird remains become, until the Jurassic period is reached when there is only one recognised species.

The earliest recognisable bird remains come from the Upper Jurassic limestone rocks of Bavaria, which were laid down in lagoon-like conditions some 150 million years ago. In 1861 quarrymen working these lithographic limestone deposits, which were already famous for their fine fossils, found an unfamiliar fossil in a split slab. This was sent to Herman von Mayer, who identified the specimen as the impression of an avian feather, and named it *Archaeopteryx lithographica*. Shortly after, an incomplete skeleton was unearthed which showed some remarkable features. The interest in this primitive bird, which was osteologically close to some of the small dinosaurs, but had well preserved feather impressions on the slab was purchased by The British Museum in 1862. There are now five known skeletons of *Archaeopteryx*, all varying in their completeness, the best being housed in Berlin.

Probably more has been written about the London and Berlin specimens than any other fossils. Some earlier workers considered that these two differed enough to warrant different names and the Berlin animal was renamed *Archaeornis*. One worker went even further, and suggested that *Archaeopteryx* gave rise to the ratites and *Archaeornis* the carinates. While no present-day worker would support his argument, many now feel that the differences between the specimens requires at least another species.

It is fortunate that the feather impressions of *Archaeopteryx*

153

are preserved for without them it would be almost impossible to identify the bones as avian. From information gathered from all of the material, one can say that *Archaeopteryx* was a bird about the size of a crow, able to perch, but with very limited powers of flight. From the geology of the area it can be said that it lived in or about the 'trees' encircling the lagoons and shallow seas that were present in that area of Germany at that period.

From the skeletons it can be seen that these primitive birds were very similar to some of the more lightly built dinosaurs, especially the coelurosaurs which were carnivorous bipeds. There are rows of small, lizard-like teeth in both the upper and lower jaws quite unlike any modern bird. The remainder of the skull also shows features more akin to the reptiles. The bones of the hand and wrist, normally so characteristic of birds, is unfused, but the number of elements is reduced. Along the leading edge of the wing, however, are three well-developed fingers, which were almost certainly used for climbing. These fingers have been lost in modern birds except for the Hoatzin chick which has a small digit that enables it to climb. A vestigial claw can also be found in many rails.

Flight feathers are well developed in *Archaeopteryx* with eight primaries and ten secondaries, but there is no evidence of a breast keel bone in any of the specimens which probably means that the bird had very limited powers of flight. The hind limb is also reduced from the basic reptile pattern, and has three toes forward and one back. The femur is reptilian probably indicating an ability to run quickly, as in many dinosaurs. But of all the reptile-like characteristics the most obvious is the long bony tail, comprised of individual vertebrae. In modern birds the vertebrae of the tail are reduced to form a short pygostyle ('parson's nose') to which the feathers are attached.

Clearly, it is still not obvious what part *Archaeopteryx* plays in the story of evolution from the pre-avis. It is certainly the first bird, but is it on the main line to recent birds? Though it must be classed as a bird because of its feathers it could be an offshoot from the pre-avis and not on the direct line to modern birds.

A further 30 million years have to pass, which is well into the Cretaceous period (135–170 million years ago), before any further avian remains are found. This material is very scanty indeed, and consists of feathers from Australia, a thigh-bone from France (attributed to a goose-like bird, *Gallornis*); an incomplete humerus named *Wyleyia* from the Weald Clay of England, whose taxonomic position is uncertain and *Enaliornis*, which was a diving bird, found in the Cambridge Greensand. These odd bones are obviously not representative of the birds which must have existed during the early part of the Cretaceous period and much more field work needs to be done before any real idea of the fauna can be acquired.

Towards the end of the Cretaceous period, birds (or at least their remains) became more common, and included *Hesperornis* and *Ichthyornis* from the chalk deposits of Kansas. *Hesperornis* was a very specialised aquatic bird, not unlike the modern diver, but had true teeth, was completely flightless and was over six feet in length. *Ichthyornis*, on the other hand, must have been a capable flier and probably resembled a small gull or large tern standing about eight inches high. Other water birds are also represented at this time and included the possible early relatives of the grebes, cormorants, flamingoes, rails and waders.

Land birds are, however, very rare and only three forms are known. There are two shoulder girdle bones, which are said to be pigeon-like from Wyoming; from Alberta a lower jaw, which is continuously being shifted from the reptiles to the birds and back, but at present is thought to be from a giant ostrich-like bird; and a couple of leg bones from Transylvania which can be attributed to the owls.

Although some primitive birds closely resemble modern species, that does not necessarily mean that they are related. If a certain mode of life is successful, which necessitates a particular body form, then this structure is likely to be evolved more than once. This is called 'convergence' and good example of this phenomenon in the living birds is between the Diving Petrel of the southern oceans and Little Auk of the northern Arctic seas. Until recently, it was believed that most of the divergence into our living orders occurred during the early Eocene, but from present studies it is possible that at least some of these orders were represented towards the end of the Cretaceous period.

The next 10 million years on the geological time-scale is referred to as the Palaeocene (70–60 million years ago) which for convenience sake will be included with the Eocene (60–40 million years ago). Very few species have been found in the Palaeocene, but towards the end of the latter period only ten of the normally recognised orders of today's birds are not represented. The absent forms are the tinamous, emus, cassowaries, kiwis, grebes, parrots, colies, trogons, nightjars and woodpeckers.

From increasing evidence it is obvious that the Eocene had a rich and varied avifauna even in its early stages. Coincident with this increase of birds of a modern type, this period produced its own highly specialised forms which were destined to become extinct at the end of the Tertiary (Caenozoic) era. A good example of this is *Odontopteryx toliapica*, found in the London Clay deposits of the Thames Estuary, which belongs to a group of pelecaniform-like birds commonly referred to as the false-toothed birds. The most remarkable feature of these birds is the tooth-like projections on both the jaws. The group died out during the Miocene or Pliocene period, but before doing so had produced a gigantic sea bird with a wing span of over sixteen feet.

Large running birds also made an appearance and are placed in their own order, the Diatrymiformes. The most complete skeleton of this type of bird was found in the Lower Eocene of Wyoming, and was named *Diatryma steini*. It probably stood at least seven feet tall, had an enormous hooked bill and in general body shape resembled the Cassowary. What the large bill was used for is rather uncertain. Some people feel that it was for tearing flesh, but huge bills of this kind could be used for cutting vegetation.

The next period, known as the Oligocene (40–25 million years ago) continued to produce a modern type fauna, and about a quarter of the present-day bird families were represented. From various parts of the world, the first petrels, gannets, falcons, guans, seriemas and plovers occur. The most spectacular group to arise during this time was another giant running bird, the phororhuscids. This group paralleled the diatrymids and had even larger hooked bills.

The following part of the Tertiary, the Miocene, occurred between 25 and 12 million years ago. This period showed the same trend as previous periods towards modern birds. Over one third of the animals recorded are sufficiently similar to recent birds to be placed in the same genera, and include seabirds, herons, ducks, birds of prey, gamebirds, bustards, waders, owls, parrots, finches and crows. At the same time grebes and woodpeckers made their first appearance.

Penguins are well represented and some fifteen types have been described the largest of which, *Anthropornis*, attained a height of some five feet. Other forms which appear to have reached their zenith at this time were the false-toothed birds and the giant phororhuscids from the New World.

157

The last of the Tertiary periods, the Pliocene, occurred between 12 and 2½ million years ago. Of all the fossil birds described from this period at least seventy-five per cent have been assigned to living genera, and in some cases the remains are virtually indistinguishable from living species. During this period the auks paralleled the penguins in becoming flightless and have been named *Mancalla* and are known from the Californian Pliocene.

Although the ratites have always been regarded as primitive it is not until this period that we find good examples of ostriches, emus, rheas and tinamous.

The Pleistocene period, often referred to as the Great Ice Age, took place about 2½ million to 10,000 years ago. The majority of species described at this time can certainly be attributed to living genera if not species. Recent forms which appear for the first time are diving petrels, ospreys, magapodes, turkeys, button-quails, jacanas, phalaropes, nightjars, hummingbirds, bee-eaters, hoopoes, puffbirds, barbets and toucans.

Once again, giant forms were produced at this time. In the Mediterreanean there was a giant swan and a vulture; a seven-foot stork is recorded from Java and another large stork from the Rancho La Brea in California. The latter locality provided the largest of all flying birds, which was the giant cathartid vulture *Teratornis*, one species of which is thought to have had a wing-span of over fourteen feet. Other evidence of gigantism has been found in the Bahamas where a large tytonid owl has been described; in New Zealand there is evidence of an enormous eagle and flightless goose.

All of the ratite families were represented at this period. Extinct emus, cassowaries, rheas and ostriches have been found in deposits of this age. Ostriches especially, are now known to have been widespread and their remains have been found in

China, eastern Europe, India and North Africa. Two large
extinct groups are also known from deposits in New Zealand
(the moas) and Madagascar (the elephant birds) which were
both destined to die out before historical times.

A Bird-watcher's calendar

Alan Vittery

Winter is traditionally the wildfowler's season: today, happily, the ducks and geese are more often sought with binoculars than shotguns.

Early January brings the International Census of Wildfowl, a co-ordinated count covering the whole of Europe and recently extended to parts of North Africa and Asia. The high density of bird-watchers in Britain makes our contribution to this exercise of particular importance; almost every wetland of significance can be covered every year, making possible the computation of relatively minor changes in a species' status. Such information, compiled over a number of years, provides scientists with a useful ecological early warning system. It also provides some of the evidence necessary for the protection of important sites from industrial and urban encroachment.

Peregrine at Work

It is wildfowl, too, that are the principal winter attraction at Slimbridge. The Wildfowl Trust is able to offer the visitor the unique combination of an unrivalled collection of world wildfowl plus the magnificent sight of thousands of White-fronted Geese and Wigeon feeding on the 'Dumbles'—the River

Severn's grassy flood plain. From the tower hide a Peregrine can often be seen at work, an increasingly rare experience in these islands in spite of recent encouraging news of breeding.

In recent years there has been the added attraction of a herd of wild Bewick's Swans wintering within the enclosures of the Trust. Such detailed observations have been possible that the (winter) lives of some individuals in the herd have been charted over a number of years.

Cold Snap

If the British bird populations are fairly static in January and February, there is nevertheless more than enough to keep the ornithologist fully active in the foreshortened days. Winter flocks of finches offer ideal opportunities for ringers to do useful work before they are diverted by the more exciting prospect of trapping migrants. On the reserves there is maintenance work to be done; ditch clearing, fence repairing and so on. But a sudden cold snap may bring large numbers of northern birds south. Sea duck and the odd diver will be found on inland reservoirs, large flights of Lapwings and Skylarks move over on a broad front, the coastal watcher may be rewarded with Snow Buntings and Shore Larks and, with luck, Waxwings will grace garden berry bushes to the delight of the town dweller. By late February the rookeries will be occupied regardless of the weather, but a false spring will often induce other species to anticipate the breeding season particularly, it would seem, in towns and cities.

First Bird of Spring

Early March finds bird-watchers expectant, but their expectations are rarely fulfilled. It is likely that the bobbing white rump of the first Wheatear, so eagerly awaited, will be denied them until the third week of the month unless they are fortunate enough to live within reach of the south coast itself. But there is nevertheless abundant evidence that the bird community is stirring. Large coastal movements of ducks and waders and the occupation of upland breeding territories are but two examples. It is sometimes difficult to separate the genuine early summer migrants, for instance the Chiffchaffs and Blackcaps, from birds which may have wintered in south-west England, Ireland or even further north. But Garganey regularly appear in the second week of the month and late March 'falls' often include such clear cut migrants as Sand Martins and Ring Ouzels. Such arrivals may also be accompanied by Stonechats and Black Redstarts of continental origin.

Cuckoo in April

Notwithstanding the vagaries of the British climate, April has deservedly acquired a reputation for being more unpredictable than other months. Summer visitors crossing to these islands in favourable conditions may be rapidly confronted with inclement weather in the form of gales or even snowstorms. The urge to establish territories drives the males of the species on, however, and the spearhead of this annual assault is usually well established before the month is out. Swallows should be more or less widespread by the second or third week and Cuckoos will be making their presence known by mid-month, although the annual competition to claim the first will have produced many bogus (and perhaps a few genuine) records before this. The hirundines, because of their exclusively insectivorous diet, are restricted to the vicinity of water during the post-arrival period and the return to traditional nesting sites may therefore be delayed for a week or two, depending on conditions.

The descending trill of the Willow Warbler will be an increasingly familiar sound as April draws on. The males of this species are highly vocal while still on passage and during a massive immigration it is quite usual for birds to be heard in towns and small suburban gardens. On the coasts Sandwich Terns pave the way for other members of their family, none of which winter in British waters. A steady passage towards breeding grounds is evident along the English Channel and both the North Sea and Atlantic shores. The marshes are again enlivened by the brilliant hue of the male Yellow Wagtail whose beauty takes one by surprise year after year.

Mass Arrivals of May

The heaviest arrivals of migrants probably take place during the latter part of April and early May. This period also accounts for the first of the latecomers such as Swifts (like the hirundines, often restricted to wetlands before dispersal to nesting sites), Garden Warblers and Turtle Doves. Bird song is at its height and nesting activity increases in intensity with the lengthening days. The hordes of immigrants bring with them two interesting categories of migrant—the transients on their way to breeding grounds in Scandinavia and the Arctic Circle (mainly waders such as Little Stints and Curlew Sandpipers), and the 'overshooters' from continental breeding ranges to the south. The former are far less numerous in spring than in autumn but the quality of their dress more than compensates for their relative scarcity. The latter occur mainly during spells of settled anticyclonic weather and south coast and East Anglian stations, in particular, can look forward with some optimism to the appearance of a Little Bittern, Purple Heron or perhaps a Bee-eater.

Rare Breeders

Occurrences of Red-footed Falcons in the south of England during this period are arguably becoming too regular to be attributable to this phenomenon. One of the alternative possibilities, the arrival of prospective breeding birds, should keep June watchers even more alert than usual. Britain, in fact, boasts a remarkable success story over the last twenty years or so in the field of attracting new and rare species to nest within our shores. The Avocet (see plate, p 143) symbolises (literally) the RSPB's achievements and the Loch Garten Ospreys are automatically national news from their first arrival to the successful rearing of the young. More recently the Fetlar Snowy Owls have captured the public's imagination and the Lake District Golden Eagles are not lagging far behind. Less dramatic in all but a purely ornithological sense has been the establishment of a healthy breeding population of Black-tailed Godwits, re-colonisation by Ruffs and Savi's Warblers, colonisation by Cetti's Warblers, Serins and Mediterranean Black-headed Gulls and the perhaps isolated discovery of a pair of Bluethroats on Speyside (see plate, p 144).

Wryneck Turnabout

On the debit side it is becoming ever more difficult to locate breeding pairs of Red-backed Shrike, Woodlark and Wryneck, although all three species are undergoing retractions of range not confined to our country. Wrynecks, at least, have added to the already considerable attraction of a June visit to the Spey valley by establishing themselves there. It is not only border-line cases which suffer changes in fortune, however.

Until a very short time ago summer lanes resounded with the cheery rattle of the Whitethroat. In one winter, for reasons not fully understood, the population of the species was decimated. On present evidence, recovery is likely to be a slower process than that which replaced many of our resident birds within a matter of a few seasons following the disaster inflicted by the winter of 1962–3. The charting of these fluctuations, some of the less spectacular of which are only apparent after the careful assimilation of detailed information, provides the summer ornithologist with the exacting, but rewarding, task of Atlas work. The division of the country into ten kilometre squares and the computation of the resulting data provides us with a comprehensive picture of our ever-changing avifauna.

Seabird Summer

Census work is of particular importance at our seabird colonies, which are seriously threatened by man's pollution of the seas. Seabirds are spread out over the oceans for most of the year and it is only during the breeding season that their numbers can be accurately assessed. Useful as they are as indicators of the level of our own destructiveness, the colonies are a fine sight in their own right. They attract many casually-interested visitors and evoke a sympathetic response to the welfare of birds as a whole.

Seabirds are still prominent in the July scene. Evening flights of Manx Shearwaters from northern colonies occur on both east and west coasts. Large roosts of Arctic, Common and Sandwich Terns form on suitable estuary sandbanks and Arctic Skuas keep in close contact. A diligent observer may pick out a family party of Roseate Terns, the least common of the British nesters. Post-breeding dispersal brings fluctuating numbers of the freshwater 'marsh' terns across from the Continent. The delicate Black Terns are occasionally joined by a stray White-winged Black or even a Whiskered from farther south.

Large movements of Swifts are a feature of fine cyclonic

165

weather in July, the birds battling into strong winds often in the opposite direction to their ultimate destination. The increase in wader numbers on our coasts is another sure indication of the approach of autumn.

For the resident species August provides, or should provide, an opportunity to capitalise on abundant food supplies and the chance perhaps to raise a second brood of youngsters. The silent woodlands are testimony, however, to the weakening mating instinct. For the summer visitors, faced with unknown hardships on their long flights to winter quarters, the vital business of building up fat reserves is a full time job. The size of this energy supply may decide whether they reach Africa safely or perish in the Sahara.

Leisurely Return

For other species, notably the wildfowl, the post-nuptial moult must be completed before any thought of long-distance flying can be entertained. But for most species the return migration is a more leisurely process than the highly motivated spring drive towards breeding grounds. Adult birds, their parental responsibilities behind them, would appear to take advantage of hard-earned experience in finding their winter quarters, possibly stopping over for days at a time at localities which have afforded them favourable transit in the past. For the immature, with only a vague instinct to guide them, the journey is more hazardous and British shores consequently play host annually to a disproportionate number of the offspring of the northern breeders, such as the Little Stints and Curlew Sandpipers that were so uncommon on the spring passage.

It is usually late August before the passerines move south in any numbers; emigration of diurnal migrants can be observed at suitable points on the south coast from this time onwards,

166

building up to a peak in September and tailing off again in the second half of October. As well as one of the latecomers, the Swift is one of the first summer migrants to leave us. The last days of August will often see huge concentrations hawking for insects at fairly high altitude; hardly one will remain by the first day of September.

It is September when the bird observatories really come into their own. The resident wardens are supplemented by eager hordes of ringers and holidaying ornithologists. This is the time of the year when anything can turn up, be it a wader from North America, reported annually in ever-increasing numbers, Pectoral Sandpipers actually occur in small flocks in good years, or a vagrant warbler from Central Asia. The weather forecasts assume a new significance as the watchers await the combination of climatic factors that will contrive to drift night migrants, which are largely dependent on a clear sight of the stars for navigation, into our path.

The Autumn 'Fall'

There are conflicting theories as to the exact circumstances causing a 'fall' of disorientated migrants, but it is generally agreed that the basic requirements are clear skies over the departure area (say in Scandinavia or on the Continent) to encourage the birds to leave, followed by cloud to 'blind' them and easterly or south-easterly winds to drift them out over the North Sea. At dawn exhausted birds may drop down in thousands to the first landfall, particularly if mist or rain has forced them low over the sea.

Predominant in these spectacular falls will be species which are common enough in our own islands, Willow Warblers, Wheatears, Whinchats (see plate, p 144), Redstarts and Pied Flycatchers. But accompanying them will be small numbers of

Bluethroats, Icterine Warblers, Barred Warblers and Red-breasted Flycatchers, the last-mentioned as much as 180 degrees off course from their intended south-easterly migration from central and eastern Europe.

As coverage and use of the mist net increases, and as identification standards improve, more and more of yesterday's 'rarities' are being shown to be regular visitors to the British Isles, but 'true' rarities will continue to occur as long as birds continue to migrate.

Spectacular Movements

October is also dominated by migrants. Late autumn 'drift' migration tends to produce unusual species of more easterly origin, such as Yellow-browed Warblers and Richard's Pipits, but the really spectacular movements involve vast numbers of immigrant thrushes, finches and other birds whose crossing from Scandinavia is assisted by the easterly and north-easterly winds prevalent at this season. Blackbirds, Redwings, Field-fares, Starlings, Goldcrests, Siskins and Bramblings feature in these arrivals which, on the North Sea coasts at least, are attended by the larger gulls seeing an easy meal in land-seeking passerines too tired to avoid their clumsy lunges. Of the less common, but regular, visitors Great Grey Shrikes, Shore Larks and the first Waxwings may be looked for and, of the non-passerines, Woodcocks may appear in large numbers. If the wind is strong enough, these same conditions will induce large coastal flights of seabirds in the North Sea. The flocks of Kittiwakes and Gannets are interspersed with a regular procession of divers, skuas and sea ducks. On the Atlantic coast it is, of course, westerly gales which drive the seabirds close inshore. There can be no finer sight for the addicted 'sea-watcher' than a north-westerly gale at St Ives, on the north coast of Cornwall. Here the birds are driven into a large bay and are forced to battle out into the wind past the town's western promontory, which itself affords the observer a sheltered site. Sabine's Gulls, Grey Phalaropes and Petrels occur during these 'blows'.

Wrecks

It is perhaps November, however, which is best known for seabird 'wrecks'. The late autumn and early winter gales seem to be too much for some of the less robust oceanic species and every year, almost without exception, there are inland records of Grey Phalaropes and Leach's Petrels at large inland reservoirs such as Staines, near London and Gràfham Water, near Huntingdon. November, too, sees the arrival of the bulk of our winter goose population, although it is often late December before the few Bean Geese make an appearance. Further influxes of thrushes, continental Starlings and finches join the roving bands of resident small birds in the countryside to take advantage of the berry and seed crop; many will move on to western Europe after only a short stay. Clouds of Knot fly like wispy smoke over our estuaries and duck numbers on lakes and marshes build up towards their mid-winter peak.

By December most species have established themselves in their winter quarters and, barring a spell of unusual weather, the bird scene should be relatively static. For the ornithologist with patience the huge gull flocks are worth study; Glaucous and Iceland Gulls occur in small numbers at coastal localities (often roosting inland) and Mediterranean Gulls are faithful visitors to several favoured spots. But it is fitting to end where we began, with the last and arguably the most attractive of the wildfowl arrivals, the locally distributed Smew. The fine drake gives us his own version of a White Christmas.

Contributors

E. E. Jackson Ted is the Chief Education Officer of the Wildfowl Trust. Though based at Slimbridge his work involves a considerable amount of travel and he frequently finds himself at Caerlaverock, on the Scottish Solway, looking at Barnacle Geese. His story of the Wildfowl Trust Expedition to the breeding grounds of these Solway birds in barren Spitsbergen is as much an adventure story as one about birds. He has frequently written about wildfowl.

David Pearson Born and bred in Suffolk, David knows the splendid coast of that county as well as anyone. Every nook and cranny, every creek and runnel has been explored in the search for birds. While in the present volume he describes the fun of twenty-four hours of play, he takes his birds very seriously. At present he lives in Kenya and spends most of his spare time ringing Little Stints. This fascination with trans-Saharan migration has resulted in papers in *The Ibis* and elsewhere.

Geoffrey Beven Dr Geoffrey lives and works in south-east England and has travelled widely to watch birds. Unlike most of us he is just as happy watching the intimate behaviour of a common bird as he is in seeing a new one. The result has been a string of authoritative summaries of species appearing in journals as varied as *British Birds*, *Birds of the World*, *World of Birds* and now the Goldfinch in this book.

John Gooders Our editor, formerly a schoolmaster and lecturer, is now a professional writer on birds. He has written the definitive guides *Where to Watch Birds* and *Where to Watch Birds in Britain and Europe* and edited the massive 9-volume *Birds of the World*. He has written scripts for Anglia Television's 'Survival' series and a book on *Wildlife Photography* jointly with Eric Hosking. His latest book *Wildlife Paradises* is published by David & Charles for whom he is currently engaged on a new series of field guides to bird identification.

Jeffery Harrison Jeffery is in the forefront of the co-operation between protectionists and sportsmen that has had such beneficial effects on conservation in Britain in recent years. Through his prolific pen he has spread the word so well that to some it seems that shooters have always been on our side! Widely travelled, Dr Harrison is secretary of WAGBI and a contributor to many journals and magazines.

Leslie Brown Resident in Kenya, it is typical of Leslie that, having taken on a book on British raptors, he should decide it necessary to tour these islands tracking down both the birds and the experts. Already the acknowledged authority on the world's birds of prey, and the co-author of the monumental *Eagles, Hawks and Falcons of the World*, Leslie is a full-time writer on birds and natural history.

J. J. Flegg Jim Flegg, PhD, is the Director of the British Trust for Ornithology and has helped that body to become a formidable go-ahead organisation that truly represents the ideal of its founders—to provide the organisation that enables amateur ornithologists to best contribute to co-operative research. Jim has written several books and contributed to many others.

Hans Beste Hans is a partner in a successful wildlife movie and photography team—the other partner is his wife Judy. Together they travel their native Australia in search of wild-life in a way that makes most of us green with envy. But Hans is much more than a cameraman, he observes with the trained eye of a naturalist and writes with accuracy and entertainment.

Ian Newton Dr Ian is a highly qualified zoologist and the acknowledged expert on finches (among other things). His article on Bullfinches shows the unimpassioned approach to his subject that is the hallmark of the good scientist. Dismissing traditional thinking he has been influential in approaching the Bullfinch pest in a spirit of calm and sense—what's more he reads well!

M. A. Ogilvie Malcolm works on the problems of duck, geese and particularly swans at the Wildfowl Trust at Slimbridge. He is also an editor of *British Birds* and a writer of papers, articles and books. He was a member of the Trust's expedition to Spitsbergen described by Ted Jackson in *The Land That God Forgot* and was a significant contributor to *The Swans*, the authoritative book by Sir Peter Scott.

Ian Beames Ian is a new man of an old breed. An all-round naturalist and countryman, one cannot but feel that he would have been happier in the last century than in this hyper-specialised age where we seem to have to concentrate on irrelevancies to add anything of significance. But Ian is also a wildlife photographer of note, and thus one of a very new breed. This dichotomy is evident in his updating of Selborne.

Richard Porter Dicky is the 'hard man' of the RSPB's law enforcement department and an avid Turkophile. His commitment to birds is complete and his knowledge of the migration of birds of prey in Europe acknowledged. In his work he sees the seamier side of others' approach to birds, an approach which he does his best to deter.

Cyril Walker Cyril is a professional palaeontologist with a passion for bird-watching that has turned him into an ornithologist. His ever-increasing knowledge of the fossil development of birds, and thus their evolution, is second to none. That such an apparently unappealing subject can be brought to life by the pen is a tribute to his enthusiasm and knowledge.

Alan Vittery 'Our Man in Lahore' was formerly 'Our Man in Istanbul' and destined to be our man elsewhere within a few years. Like many diplomats Alan spends his spare time watching birds, but he knows his own country as well and for eighteen months wrote the Stop-press news column of *World of Birds*. He is active in the Turkish Ornithological Society and edits their report.